The Holiness

of

G. K. Chesterton

Also published by Gracewing

The Elusive Father Brown:
The Life of Mgr John O'Connor by Julia Smith

The Holiness
of
G. K. Chesterton

Introduced and Edited by William Oddie

Freedom Publishing
AUSTRALIA

GRACEWING

First published in 2010

Gracewing
2 Southern Avenue, Leominster
Herefordshire HR6 0QF

Published in Australia
by
Freedom Publishing Pty Ltd
35 Whitehorse Road
Balwyn
Victoria 3103

UK ISBN 978 085244 725 3

Typeset by
Action Publishing Technology Ltd, Gloucester, GL1 5SR

Printed in Great Britain by the MPG Books Group, Bodmin and King's Lynn

Contents

Contributors

Dr Sheridan Gilley is a church historian and Emeritus Reader in Theology at the University of Durham, a member of the Editorial Board of *The Chesterton Review* and a Trustee of the G. K. Chesterton Institute for Faith and Culture. His best-known work is *Newman and His Age* (1990). His recent publications include the Centenary Edition of G. K. Chesterton's *Orthodoxy*, in 2008, and with Brian Stanley, the nineteenth-century volume of the *Cambridge History of Christianity*. He was President of the Ecclesiastical History Society for 2010.

Revd Dr Ian Ker is Senior Research Fellow in Theology at St Benet's Hall, Oxford and has taught both English literature and theology at universities in England and the United States. He is the author and editor of more than twenty books on Newman, including his most famous, *John Henry Newman: A Biography* (1988), which has just been reissued by the Oxford University Press. He has also written a warmly received work of popular apologetics, *Mere Catholicism*. His book *The Catholic Revival in English Literature, 1845–1961* (2003) contains a seminal chapter on Chesterton, and his biography of Chesterton will be published by the Oxford University Press in 2011.

Nicholas Madden is a Discalced Carmelite priest, resident in Dublin. He studied in Carmelite houses, University College, Dublin, the Teresianum, Rome and Durham University, from which he holds a Ph.D. in Patristics. He still has a toehold in the Maynooth Patristic Symposium, the proceedings of which he attends and to which he contributes. He spent most of his religious life in formation houses of the Order.

Revd Dr Aidan Nichols OP is the former Prior, and is presently Sub-Prior, of Blackfriars, Cambridge and a member of the Cambridge University Divinity faculty. He was the first John Paul II Memorial Visiting Lecturer at Oxford University, where he gave a series of lectures on the theology of G. K. Chesterton. He has been described as the world's most prolific theologian: his many books include three on Hans Urs von Balthasar and *The Theology of Joseph Ratzinger: An Introductory Study* (1988); he is widely known for an influential work on religion in the modern world, *Christendom Awake* (1993). His latest work is *G. K. Chesterton, Theologian* (2009).

Dr William Oddie is a former editor of the *Catholic Herald* and fellow of St Cross College, Oxford.

Father John Saward is a fellow and associate lecturer at Blackfriars, Oxford and Parish Priest of Saint Gregory & Saint Augustine's, Oxford. He previously held the posts of Lecturer in Dogmatic Theology at St Cuthbert's College, Durham (1980–92), Professor of Systematic Theology at St Charles Borromeo Seminary in Philadelphia, Pennsylvania (1992–98), and Professor of Dogmatic Theology in the International Theological Institute, Gaming, Austria. His published works include books on Hans Urs von Balthasar and Pope John Paul II and, among others, *The Way of the Lamb: The Spirit of Childhood and the End of Age* (1999), *Cradle of Redeeming Love: The Theology of the Christmas Mystery* (2002) and *Sweet and Blessed Country: The Christian Hope for Heaven* (2005).

Fr Bob Wild, originally from the Catholic diocese of Buffalo, NY, has been a member, since 1971, of the Madonna House community founded by Catherine Doherty. He has edited many of her works, as well as writing a trilogy on her spirituality. He sees a similarity in her teaching with that of GK, as they both emphasised the extraordinary nature of the ordinary. As a member of the Ottawa Chesterton Society in the 1990s, he wrote a series of articles on Chesterton's holiness, calling for his cause of canonisation. He is nearing completion of a book, *The Tumbler of God, Chesterton as a Mystic*, expanding the theme of his chapter in the present book.

Introduction

William Oddie

Just after Chesterton's premature death at the age of sixty-two, Maisie Ward, his first biographer, a friend of thirty years, was touched by a tribute paid to him by the maid at a house he used to visit in his home town of Beaconsfield. With tears in her eyes, she said simply 'Oh Miss, our Mr Chesterton dying – he was a sorter saint Miss, wasn't he – just to look at him when you handed him his hat made you feel sorter awesome.'[1]

It has not always been as evident, even to many of his admirers, that he was 'a sorter saint'; to others, though, like the late Cardinal Emmett Carter, who described him on the fiftieth anniversary of his death as one of those 'holy lay persons' who 'have exercised a truly prophetic role within the Church and the world', it has been clear enough. Cardinal Carter did not then (though later he changed his mind) believe that it would be possible to introduce a cause for his ultimate canonisation, since he did 'not think that we are sufficiently emancipated from certain concepts of sanctity'[2] to be able to contemplate such a thing. Cardinal Carter's homily, when published in the *Chesterton Review*, inspired the English historian J. J. Scarisbrick to wonder, despite the Cardinal's remarks, whether there were not, in fact, 'good grounds for considering Gilbert Keith Chesterton for canonisation'.

---

[1] Maisie Ward, *Return to Chesterton*, London and New York, Sheed & Ward, 1952, p. 261.

[2] 'Homily for the Mass of the Anniversary of the Death of G. K. Chesterton', *The Chesterton Review*, vol. xii, n. 4, November 1986, 439.

We all know that he was an enormously good man as well as an enormous one. My point is that he was more than that. There was a special integrity and blamelessness about him, a special devotion to the good and to justice ... Above all, there was that breathtaking, intuitive (almost angelic) possession of the Truth and awareness of the supernatural which only a truly holy person can enjoy. This was the gift of heroic intelligence and understanding – and of heroic prophecy. He was a giant, spiritually as well as physically. Has there ever been anyone quite like him in Catholic history?[3]

It is certainly time to ask why this should be, as undoubtedly it is, a growing view: after a paper I delivered in 2008 to the annual conference of the American Chesterton Society, I was asked what stage the cause towards Chesterton's beatification had reached in England. When I said there *was* no cause, the audience showed signs of incredulity. I explained lamely that there had to be evidence of a cult: one man stood up and said, indicating the approximately 500 present, 'what the heck do they think *we* are?' The English audience at the conference on 'The Holiness of G. K. Chesterton' held in Oxford the following year (the papers delivered at this conference form the core of the present volume) responded in a similar way. Certainly, there has been for many years a cult of Gilbert Chesterton in countries as distant from each other as Italy and Argentina. A few months after the Chesterton Society's 2009 conference, a prayer for his intercession emerged, which when posted on the Society's blog quickly inspired translations in both Italian and Spanish (texts in appendix B).

Before we pursue the question of Chesterton's holiness, nevertheless, we need to ask again why such a notion should still be unthinkable to so many. Perhaps it is necessary to share his own simplicity and purity of heart to begin to perceive it with the clarity of that housemaid. To the clever and sophisticated, commentators like A. N. Wilson, the very idea is absurd: he recently dismissed the 'bizarre talk of GK's canonisation' with the impatience of all those who admire Chesterton as a wit and perhaps even as a

---

[3.] *The Chesterton Review*, vol. xii, no. 4, November 1986, 584.

perceptive (but lightweight) social critic, but who wish to close their minds firmly against any notion of his virtue, let alone his holiness. Chesterton, on this reading, cannot bear the weight of any very close scrutiny, either of his thought or of his personality: 'with so playful a writer as Chesterton, one needs to tread carefully', as Wilson puts it.

With all this goes another assertion, common among those who like Chesterton well enough but are anxious to underplay the significance of his pilgrimage from agnosticism to theism to a kind of Unitarianism then on to Anglican Catholicism and finally to Rome; and especially of that final and definitive stage of his spiritual journey. The implication is sometimes made that after he became a Roman Catholic, his writing deteriorated; even that he became a mere polemical hack in the service of his Church. Thus, for the Anglican A. L. Maycock the decade beginning in 1904, 'The decade of *Heretics* and *Orthodoxy*, of "The Ballad of the White Horse", of … the *Charles Dickens*, the first two volumes of Father Brown, of *The Victorian Age in Literature* and much else shows him at the summit of his powers.'[4] The view, nevertheless, that Chesterton reached the summit only after his reception into the Catholic Church in 1922, with The *Everlasting Man, St Francis* and, above all perhaps, with *St Thomas Aquinas*, is probably more generally held. Etienne Gilson, one of the most substantial Thomist scholars of the last century, famously remarked on the appearance of *St Thomas Aquinas* that 'Chesterton makes one despair. I have been studying St Thomas all my life and I could never have written such a book.'[5] Despite so massive an intellectual achievement as *St Thomas Aquinas,* nevertheless, the notion of Chesterton as a thinker continued to face exactly the same objection after his death as the more far-reaching perception that he was a saint. How could anyone so exuberantly funny be a thinker, let alone an exemplar of holiness?

[4] A. L. Maycock, *The Man who was Orthodox*, London, D. D. Dobson, 1963, p. 11.
[5] Maisie Ward, *Gilbert Keith Chesterton*, London, Sheed and Ward, 1944, p. 525.

Another kind of objection entirely has to be confronted: the recurrent accusation that, as Adam Gopnik put it in the *New Yorker* magazine, not only was Chesterton an anti-Semite, he had an 'ugly' and 'obsessive' hatred of Jews: he was, in short, 'a *nasty* anti-Semite and medievalising reactionary' who needs to be protected 'from his admirers, who *pretend* that he was not' [my italics]. I believe that this accusation is not only ignorant but preposterous, and that there is evidence (some of it new) not only that Chesterton throughout his life, whatever his scathing opinions on certain individual Jews, was generally positive in his views on Jews and Jewry, and outraged over anti-Jewish persecutions, whether Czarist, anti-Dreyfusard or Nazi. I have, therefore thought it necessary to deal with the accusation of anti-Semitism, and have done so in an Appendix.

Resistance to any notion of Chesterton's holiness has taken many forms. Such resistance, even in the case of servants of God whose sanctity now seems almost unassailable, is hardly unprecedented, and not only in secularist quarters. It is worthwhile to remember, perhaps, that difficult though it now is to imagine, until comparatively recently the sanctity of John Henry Newman was very far from being universally acknowledged, not only by literary intellectuals, for whom such questions do not arise, or (very differently) by members of the Anglican Church, which had so frequently felt the polemical sting of this most brilliant and witty controversialist, but also by Roman Catholics. As late as the 1950s, many Catholics thought of Newman as a great theologian but not as a particularly holy man. For most of the seventy years following Newman's death there was no cult, even at the Birmingham Oratory where his life as a Catholic had been lived out.

Have we now, seventy-three years after Chesterton's death, reached a kind of tipping point in his reputation, of the same kind that Newman's reputation reached, leading to the opening of his cause in 1959, seventy-eight years after his death? It is no idle question: for, in the words of the Prefect of the Congregation for the Causes of Saints, Cardinal Saraiva Martins , 'If for the faithful [there is] no reputation of holiness, the bishop cannot even initiate the cause.'[6] Is there, and if there is not should there be, such a reputation?

To begin at the beginning, how do we know a saint when we see one? John Henry Newman once expressed his dislike of hagiographies which in his words 'chop up a Saint into chapters of faith, hope and charity'. The danger, he thought, was the creation of a notion of sanctity which was somehow bland and conformist. He pointed out that the saints of the early church 'rather than writing formal doctrinal trea-tises ... write controversy'. Not only that, they 'mix up their own persons ... with the didactic or polemical works which engaged them'.[7] Newman could almost have been writing about himself; he could also have been describing someone as yet unborn: Chesterton denied that he was a real novelist by saying that he 'could not be a novelist; because I really like to see ideas or notions wrestling naked ... and not dressed up in a masquerade as men and women. But I could be a journalist because I could not help being a controversialist';[8] and we might add that if anyone in the modern age ever, in Newman's words, mixed up his 'own [person] ... with the didactic or polemical works which engaged [him]' more than Chesterton did, it is difficult to know who it might be.

The saints of the early church were controversialists; but though Newman may have disliked their being 'chopped up into chapters of faith, hope and charity', they could hardly have been saints without these cardinal virtues: indeed, they became controversialists because of them. Chesterton was a controversialist because of his passion for the truth, because he had a real hatred of false thinking, of what he, following the Christian tradition, called 'heresy': his discovery of the Christian religion was achieved with an intellectual rigour which we can say is the hallmark of all his great writings, a category which includes much of his journalism. And though Chesterton never flaunted his personal faith in his writings, his passionate commitment to it could emerge at any time. At one of his frequent speaking engagements

6. http://www.zenit.org/article-15716?l=english
7. Newman, *Historical Sketches*, London, Longmans, Green & Co., 1897, p. 84.
8. *Autobiography*, London, Fisher Press, 1992, p. 298.

a Canon Barnett recalled that a member of the audience 'spoke discourteously of Christ':

> Mr Chesterton [recalled Canon Barnett] bore him for the allotted time, and then slipping off his indifference like a loose coat, sprang to his feet and, with glorious eloquence and rapidity, told of his own faith, stripped the incidents of time and circumstance from the Character which has transfigured history, and declaimed that reverence and humility were the paths all men should keep open, for they alone led to the evolution of the true. I never now read anything by Mr. Chesterton without seeing him on that platform defending, in a physical elephantine rage, his spiritual angelic surety.[9]

And this 'spiritual angelic surety' was intellectually decisive: it governed absolutely his thinking about everything, whether he was unambiguously writing about religion or not. As he put it in December 1903, very early in his career as a writer,

> You cannot evade the issue of God; whether you talk about pigs or the binomial theory, you are still talking about Him ... Things can be irrelevant to the proposition that Christianity is false, but nothing can be irrelevant to the proposition that Christianity is true. Zulus, gardening, butcher's shops, lunatic asylums, housemaids and the French Revolution – all these things not only may have something to do with the Christian God, but must have something to do with Him if He really lives and reigns.[10]

His perceptions of the real world and everything in it had already been transformed by his new faith: as he had put it earlier that year, after conversion, 'With this idea once inside our heads a million things become transparent as if a lamp were lit behind them.'[11]

So, we can say that his faith was the rocklike foundation of his thought. We can say, too, that his whole life exempli-

---

[9.] Maisie Ward, *Return to Chesterton*, p. 75.

[10.] 'A Universal Relevance', *The Daily News*, 12 December 1903.

[11.] 'The Return of the Angels', *The Daily News*, 14 March 1903.

fied the virtue of hope; indeed, it defined him as a writer in a century increasingly engulfed by hopelessness. And we can say that what he called pessimism – for him a key word – was one of the few things that could rouse him to real anger, to controversy which had about it a fierce and personal tinge. Nowhere do we see this more clearly than in an attack he launched as early as 1901 on Schopenhauer, that great philosopher of absolute loss of all hope:

> In the case of Schopenhauer, tinging all the heavens with his own tremendous mood, it is inevitable that we should speak personally. And of all men whose souls have influenced the world, Schopenhauer seems to me the most contemptible. … In his most famous essay, 'The Misery of Life', he moans that 'every satisfied wish begets a new one,' which seems to me the definition of happiness … Schopenhauer positively complains of the fact that the heart is 'a bottomless abyss', as if to find a bottom to it would not be the end of all human hope.[12]

And 'human hope' was for him not simply a personal possession, though it was that at the very least: it was a cause, passionately believed in and fought for. From the beginning, as a writer, as he wrote later in the *Autobiography*, he was 'full of a new and fiery resolution to write against the Decadents and the Pessimists who ruled the culture of the age'.[13] But he had begun to react strongly against 'the Pessimists' long before he became a journalist: for, the fashionable pessimism and languor of the *fin de siecle* transgressed against what became – after he had emerged from what we can without exaggeration call the dark night of the soul through which he lived during his time at the Slade School of Art (autumn 1893 to summer 1894) – the most powerful motivating perception of his whole life: that is, his gratitude for all creation, and particularly for his own life. 'Pessimism' encapsulated what was for him the cardinal sin of ingratitude: in a notebook dating from the autumn

---

[12.] 'The Great Pessimist', *The Daily News*, 7 June 1906.
[13.] *Autobiography*, p. 92.

of 1894 (he was just twenty) he penned a two-line pensée headed 'A pessimist', which read simply:

> So you criticise the cosmos
> And borrow a skull and a tongue to do it with.[14]

When Chesterton collected a number of his pieces into a book, which he entitled *The Defendant*, he made it clear that the attack on pessimism was for him a major theme of the collection. In his Introduction, he asserts that in the modern age,

> Pessimism is now patently, as it always was essentially, more commonplace than piety ... The pessimist is commonly spoken of as the man in revolt. He is not. Firstly, because it requires some cheerfulness to continue in revolt, and secondly, because pessimism appeals to the weaker side of everybody, and the pessimist, therefore, drives as roaring a trade as the publican. The person who is really in revolt is the optimist, who generally lives and dies in a desperate and suicidal effort to persuade all the other people how good they are.[15]

In defending what he called the 'discredited' virtue of humility, he took the opportunity 'to remark that this discredit has arisen at the same time as a great collapse of joy in current literature and philosophy. Men have revived the splendour of Greek self-assertion at the same time that they have revived the bitterness of Greek pessimism'.[16]

His optimism was not something into which he had to argue himself: for most of his life, once he had finally and definitively emerged from the profoundly depressive feelings of the Slade period,[17] it was something which entirely

---

[14]. BL MS Add. 73334 f5.

[15]. G. K. Chesterton, *The Defendant*, London, J. M. Dent, 1901, pp. 2–4.

[16]. Chesterton, 'In defence of humility,' ibid., p. 99.

[17]. It has become normal to define this period of depressive feelings by referring to his revulsion against what he understood of the theory of impressionism as it was understood at the Slade School of Art: but in fact he was only at the Slade for one year, and the depressions went on for at least two years and probably longer, though they certainly ended at about the time he made his decision to discontinue his studies there. See my *Chesterton and the Romance of Orthodoxy*, pp. 89ff.

possessed him. And once he had become a Christian, it informed and defined his faith. 'Christianity' he wrote in 1908, 'satisfies suddenly and perfectly man's ancestral instinct for being the right way up; satisfies it supremely in this; that by its creed joy becomes something gigantic and sadness something special and small.' And of course, because Chesterton is always a sign of contradiction, that means also that at the heart of any opposing world-view, ancient or modern, is despair.

> To the pagan ... the small things are as sweet as the small brooks breaking out of the mountain; but the broad things are as bitter as the sea. When the pagan looks at the very core of the cosmos he is struck cold. Behind the gods, who are merely despotic, sit the fates, who are deadly ... It is profoundly true that the ancient world was more modern than the Christian. The common bond is in the fact that ancients and moderns have both been miserable about existence, about everything, while mediaevals were happy about that at least. I freely grant that the pagans, like the moderns, were only miserable about everything – they were quite jolly about everything else. I concede that the Christians of the Middle Ages were only at peace about everything – they were at war about everything else.[18]

* * *

Chesterton's intellect, then, was entirely suffused by his faith; and his heart was filled by a hope that welled up from his unfailing gratitude for the gift of life. As for his charity, we can say that Schopenhauer was one of the very few exceptions that prove the rule: nowhere in general do we see it more clearly than in his love for his intellectual opponents, especially for Shaw: 'Nothing could have been more generous', wrote Shaw after his death, 'than his treatment of me'.[19] He was a controversialist because he hated heresy; but he had an extraordinary capacity for loving the heretic: he might even have come to love Schopenhauer if

[18.] *The Collected Works of G. K. Chesterton*, I, San Francisco, Ignatius Press, 1986, p. 14.

[19.] Michael Holroyd, *Bernard Shaw, The One-Volume Definitive Edition*, London, Chatto and Windus, 1997, p. 373.

they had actually met, as he did frequently meet Shaw and Wells: he might even have cheered him up. In controversy, no matter how fierce, as Belloc wrote after his death, 'He seemed always to be in a mood not only of comprehension for his opponent but of admiration for some quality in him ... it was this in him which made him, with other qualities, so universally beloved.'[20]

This was a quality that Chesterton shared with other holy men; it is, indeed, one of the reasons he understood them so well, a clear example of what is termed 'connaturality', the faculty by which one holy man has a special insight into the mind and heart of another; St Thomas Aquinas's huge productivity, he wrote, could not have been achieved 'if he had not been thinking even when he was not writing; but above all thinking combatively. This, in his case, certainly did not mean bitterly or spitefully or uncharitably; but it did mean combatively. As a matter of fact, it is generally the man who is not ready to argue, who is ready to sneer. That is why, in recent literature, there has been so little argument and so much sneering'.[21]

Like St Thomas, Chesterton was both combative and charitable; like him, too, he was constantly 'thinking even when he was not writing': One of his friends once saw him

> emerge from Shoe Lane, hurry into the middle of Fleet Street, and abruptly come to a standstill in the centre of the traffic. He stood there for some time, wrapped in thought, while buses, taxis and lorries eddied about him in a whirlpool and while drivers exercised to the full their gentle art of expostulation. Having come to the end of his meditations, he held up his hand ... and returned to Shoe lane.[22]

His legendary absent-mindedness, according to Ian Crowther, demonstrates that 'here was a true contemplative, given (as few people are) to the habit of prolonged and concentrated thought'.[23]

---

20. Hilaire Belloc in *The Observer*, 21 June 1936.
21. G. K. Chesterton, *Collected Works*, II, p. 499.
22. Maisie Ward, *Return to Chesterton*, pp. 72–3.
23. Ian Crowther, *Chesterton*, London, Claridge, 1991, p. 11.

If he was a contemplative, was he also a mystic, as Maisie
Ward believed (asserting that *The Everlasting Man* and *St.
Francis* seemed to her 'the highest expression of Gilbert's
mysticism')? She added that she had 'hesitated to use the
word for it is not one to be used lightly, but I can find no
other'.[24] There are at least two very clear views on the
question of whether or not Chesterton was a mystic, represented in this volume by Fr Nicholas Madden OCD and Fr
Bob Wild. Was he a true mystic in the classical sense, in the
same sense as St John of the Cross or St Teresa of Avila were?
Fr Madden, writing from within the same tradition, argues
(chapter four) that there is little support for such a view in
his published writings:

> The grasp, the insight, the originality, the delight, mark every-
> thing he expressed, his detective stories, his controversial
> writing, his biographies, his conversation with children, his
> brilliance as a debater, his poetry, his faith in search of under-
> standing ... Chesterton was undoubtedly a man of capacious
> spirit, but realizations are not encounters and encounters with
> the divine seem to be at the core of Christian mysticism in its
> strictest sense.[25]

Certainly, we cannot, as Father Madden says says, 'equate
Chesterton's contemplation with mental prayer'. But there
was undoubtedly, as I hope to show, at least one docu-
mented 'encounter', and probably more. What it may be
true to say, as Fr Bob Wild argues (chapter five), is that
he was 'a new *kind* of mystic'; perhaps it was by being, as
Marshall McLuhan (a deeply perceptive commentator on
Chesterton) argued,[26] a 'practical mystic'; I shall return to
McLuhan's view presently.

Whether he was a true 'mystic' or not, he was undoubtedly
a thinker, though on his death, the *Manchester Guardian*'s
obituary made a point of dismissing the widespread use of

[24.] Maisie Ward, *Gilbert Keith Chesterton*, London, Sheed & Ward, 1944,
pp. 410–11.
[25.] See below, p. 73.
[26.] Marshall McLuhan, 'G. K. Chesterton: A Practical Mystic', *Dalhousie
Review*, 15 (4), 1936, 455–6.

the word 'philosopher' to describe Chesterton as 'very ill-chosen'. He had, asserted the writer, 'a profusion of fresh and original ideas, but they owed more to ... an enormously zestful temperament than to continuous or connected thought'. His friend Belloc commented that 'The intellectual side of him has been masked for many and for some hidden by his delight in the exercise of words and especially in the comedy of words.' But there was nothing merely facetious about his delight in the comedy of life. Belloc called it the 'constant and exuberant geniality which all around him ... felt at once, and feelings were in a sense nourished' and explained it as a 'genius for good humour lifted to the plane on which it becomes a moving and efficient virtue'. 'The importance of humour', argues Fr Ker (p. 38), 'is essential both for understanding Chesterton's concept of holiness and also for appreciating his own holiness'.

Chesterton's humour is surely part of a God-centredness in his personality which can only be fully appreciated by understanding something of its origins. There is a moment in the life story of many saints in which personal crisis is followed by a moment of vision, a moment in which there is a personal encounter with God which brings about a complete change of direction. There is, I suggest, such a moment in Chesterton's life.

He was twenty years old. He had just left the Slade School of Art, where he had undergone a prolonged time of periodic depressions. After possibly the worst but certainly the last of these, he wrote to his friend Edmund Clerihew Bentley about what seemed to be – and in fact was – the final ending of this dark period in his life. We can date this letter in the summer of 1894: and in it he can only be talking about some kind of clearly and definitively religious experience: he describes it as a 'vision' and writes of 'speaking to God':

> Inwardly speaking I have had a funny time. A meaningless fit of depression, taking the form of certain absurd psychological worries, came upon me, and instead of dismissing it and talking to people, I had it out and went very far into the abysses indeed. The result was that I found that things, when examined,

necessarily spelt such a mystically satisfactory state of things, that without getting back to earth, I saw lots that made me certain it is all right. The vision is fading into common day now, and I am glad. It is embarrassing talking to God face to face, as a man speaketh to a friend [Chesterton is referring here to Exodus 33, in the Authorised Version, which he loved and knew well: 'and the Lord spake unto Moses face to face, as a man speaketh unto his friend'].[27]

After this 'vision' (which does seem to be, in Fr Madden's phrase, some kind of 'encounter with the divine') he never again fell into the depression and instability from which he had emerged. This is how he wrote about the consequences of this final emergence from 'the abysses' when he came to write his autobiography forty years later; it is a key passage:

I had wandered to a position not very far from the phrase of my Puritan grandfather, when he said that he would thank God for his creation [even] if he were a lost soul. I hung on to religion by one thin thread of thanks ... At the back of our brains ... there was a forgotten blaze or burst of astonishment at our own existence. The object of the artistic and spiritual life was to dig for this submerged sunrise of wonder; so that a man might suddenly understand that he was alive, and be happy.[28]

The rest of his life, we can say, Chesterton spent digging for that 'submerged sunrise of wonder'. The autobiography is not always a reliable source of information about Chesterton's life. But at this point there is strong contemporary evidence for its reliability. A notebook he began keeping in the autumn of that year is full of a sense of wonder and of gratitude for his own existence. Here is one of the reflections I found in it, when I was researching my book *Chesterton and the Romance of Orthodoxy*:

There is one secret for life
The secret of constant astonishment.

[27.] Ffinch, 41. BL MS Add. 73191.
[28.] *Autobiography*, pp. 91–2.

On the same page he writes this:

> There is one thing which gives radiance to everything, streets,
> houses, lamp posts, communities, politics, lives –
> It is the idea of something round the corner

At about the time he started this particular notebook, his
friends Bentley and Oldershaw went up to Oxford and other
friends went elsewhere; he undoubtedly missed them, and
he wrote a poem called 'The Idyll', which expresses his
feelings about their departure. It ends

> Two of them are at Oxford and one in Scotland and two at
> other places.
> But I wish they would all walk in now, for the tea is made.

One biographer thinks that this poem is evidence for the
theory that Chesterton was still prone to depressive feelings,
even after the vision he wrote about to Bentley. But if one
reads 'The Idyll', not in Maisie Ward's biography but on the
manuscript page, one finds this, immediately following it:

> Who said angel's tears?
> I say angels roaring with laughter
> For angels love and know say the Rabbis
> And laughter is the juncture of love & knowledge.

On the same page he wrote a series of *pensées* – brief uncon-
nected thoughts – which show a new flourishing of his
religious interests together with a newly rediscovered and
now permanent optimism, a gratitude for his own existence
and that of his fellow men, and a rejection of his former
depressive self; there is a clear sense, here and in other
writings from this period, that a corner has been turned and
that a new life is now beginning:

> It matters less what a man's religion is
> As long as it keeps ahead of him

> Charity to one's stupid old selves
> It is the only hard charity

Existence is the deepest fact we can think of
And it is such a nice fact

If I could sing the most poetical poem of my vision
I would sing the poem of Charing Cross Station

In the same notebook occurs the following, written, it is worthwhile to reflect, about fourteen years before his theological development from Agnosticism to a form of Catholic Christianity comes to its natural conclusion with *Orthodoxy*:

Have you taken in the conception
Of the tremendous Everything which is anywhere
And dreamed that it could fail to satisfy anything in you?

It is clear that we are very close here to Chesterton's first astonished discovery of what that 'Everything' was, or at least, where it came from. A few pages before, he had written a brief poem called 'A walk'. It is just three lines long:

Have you ever known what it is to walk
Along a road in such a frame of mind
That you thought you might meet God at any turn of the path?

Turning these pages one has a strong sense that in them at times Chesterton is struggling for words, almost for breath; that his direct experience of the 'sunrise of wonder' he writes about in the notebook was being recorded here for the first time; and that this first rediscovery of wonder and joy was simply beyond his powers of utterance to describe; at one point, he expresses his intense frustration:

I pause between two dark houses,
For there is a song in my heart,
If I could sing at this moment what I wish to sing,
The nations would crown me,
If I were dumb ever afterwards,
For I am sure it would be the greatest song in the world ...
But it will not come out. [My emphasis]

We can almost say that the rest of his life was spent in a more and more articulate attempt to sing that song; and after his death, in the context of his massive complete *oeuvre* (over eighty books, hundreds of poems, and many thousands of articles) one critic wrote that 'The other articles of the Chestertonian creed fall easily into place once this ruling principle of "wonder in all things" ... is firmly grasped.'

We can say, perhaps, that it is in his sense of wonder at the material world and at the gift of creation itself, in his sense of 'radiance' in 'everything, streets, houses, lamp posts, communities, politics, lives' that we can understand how Chesterton can justifiably be called 'a new kind of mystic'. It is in the way in which he can perceive and then transfigure the stuff of everyday living, for us too, by the light of his own 'sunrise of wonder', that his 'practical mysticism' can best be understood. As Marshall McLuhan explains it,

> There are two principal sides to everything, a practical side and a mystical ... It is necessary to define the sense in which Mr Chesterton is a mystic, before the relation of this to the practical side can be judged. He once wrote: 'Real mystics don't hide mysteries, they reveal them. They set a thing up in broad daylight and when you've seen it, it is still a mystery. But the mystagogues hide a thing in secrecy; and when you find it, it's a platitude.' The mysteries revealed by Mr Chesterton are the daily miracles of sense and consciousness ... Mr. Chesterton has stepped beyond the frontiers of poetry to what M. Maritain in speaking of Rimbaud calls 'the Eucharistic passion which he finds in the heart of life'.[29]

Chesterton's sense of wonder, we need to insist, derives from an absolute centredness in God, who is its always bubbling source: we can see his own perception of this reaching its natural intellectual conclusion by the end of 1903 (he was twenty-nine), in the article in *The Daily News* (already quoted) in which he explains his discovery

---

[29.] Marshall McLuhan, 'G. K. Chesterton: A Practical Mystic', *Dalhousie Review*, 455–6.

that the world, clearly examined, does point with an extreme suggestiveness, to the existence of a spiritual world, of a world of agencies, not apparently produced by matter, capable to some extent of controlling and inspiring, capable to some extent of being known ... The return to the spiritual view of life depends on no particular argument. It rests, like the movement towards evolution, on the fact that the thing works out. We put on the theory, like a magic hat, and history becomes translucent like a house of glass.[30]

And this new perspective induces in him an irrepressible lightness of spirit. This was in some ways something of a problem for him. As he put it in one of his early apologetic articles,

I have begun to realise that there are a good many people to whom my way of speaking about these things appears like an indication that I am flippant or imperfectly sincere ... I think I see the naturalness of the mistake, and how it arose in people so far removed from the Christian atmosphere. Christianity is itself so jolly a thing that it fills the possessor of it with a certain silly exuberance ...[31]

This conviction that joy is at the centre of the Christian faith is something that many have experienced at certain times: but few have held it at the centre of their lives so entirely and so exultantly until death, as Chesterton did. Towards the end of his life, he looked back on it as having been 'indefensibly happy'. We have to ask why: and the only answer I can arrive at is the same answer we have to give when we ask similar questions about the saints: that they were all, each in his or her own way, very close to God and that only that closeness can explain their lives and the irrepressible joy at the centre of them.

His friend Lucian Oldershaw told Maisie Ward that even at school, 'we felt that he was looking for God'. A friend who knew him well in the years that led up to *Orthodoxy*,

---

[30.] G. K. Chesterton, 'The return of the angels', *The Daily News*, 14 March 1903.

[31.] 'Christianity and Rationalism', *The Clarion*, 22 July 1904; *Works*, I, p. 374.

Rann Kennedy, gave her what she called 'electrifying' testimony:

> Gilbert was busy always with the other world ... We must explain him like the hermits. So obviously, burningly led by the Holy Ghost that he had no time to think of his own soul's salvation ... Gilbert had innocence, simplicity, down-in-the dirt humility he had an [exceeding] calm of soul. He enjoyed a perpetual Eucharist, the Eucharist of desire ... Gilbert [was] always busy with the other world, was ministered to by angels like Our Lord.[32]

After his death, his lifelong friend, E. C. Bentley (inventor of the clerihew), wrote of his 'exuberantly joyous and love-compelling personality'. Belloc's judgement that he was 'universally beloved' is no mere obituary cliché. At his funeral, the streets of Beaconsfield were lined with mourners: it is moving to reflect that it was the police who asked if the funeral cortege could take a longer route from the church to the cemetery, so that more people might have a chance to say goodbye. His friend William Titterton followed the coffin on foot:

> It is a roundabout way we go. For the police of the place will have it that Gilbert Chesterton shall make his last earthly journey past the homes of the people who knew him and loved him best. And there they were, crowding the pavements, and all, like us, bereaved. Yet it was almost a gala day. There was no moping, no gush of tears. Nay, there was laughter as one of us recalled him and his heroic jollity to another's ready remembrance. A policeman at the gate of the cemetery said to Edward Macdonald, 'Most of the lads are on duty, else they would all have been here.'[33]

There were of course many epitaphs. Pius XI sent a telegram describing him as a 'gifted defender of the Catholic Faith' (which sounds almost like a kind of informal declaration that he was a Doctor of the Church). 'Blessed are they that

[32.] Maisie Ward, *Return to Chesterton*, p. 237.
[33.] Michael Coren, *Gilbert: The Man Who Was Chesterton*, London, Jonathan Cape, 1989, pp. 4–5.

saw him and were honoured by his friendship', pronounced Monsignor Ronald Knox at the memorial Requiem Mass in Westminster Cathedral, two weeks after his death: 'They found in him a living example of charity, of chivalry, of unbelievable humility which will remain with them, perhaps as a more effective document of Catholic verity than any word even he wrote.'[34] But for most of those who loved him his true epitaph was the lovely verse written years before by the poet laureate, Walter de la Mare, which by the wish of his widow Frances appeared on the service sheet at his funeral Requiem Mass in Beaconsfield. Like Monsignor Knox's panegyric it recalls his chivalry; above all it depicts him as a warrior, but a warrior animated only by his love of God and of the human race:

> Knight of the Holy Ghost, he goes his way,
> Wisdom his motley, Truth his loving jest;
> The mills of Satan keep his lance in play,
> Pity and innocence his heart at rest.[35]

[34] Philip Caraman SJ (ed.), *Occasional Sermons of Ronald Knox*, London, Burns & Oates, 1960, p. 405.
[35] Maisie Ward, *Gilbert Keith Chesterton*, p. 552.

Chesterton's Sanctity:
The Spirit of Childhood and the
Metaphysics of Wonder

John Saward

When people asked Chesterton why he became a Catholic, he would tell them: 'to get rid of my sins'.[1] On first hearing, the answer seems pathetically insufficient, a throw-away line, but further consideration shows it to be perfectly satisfactory, a masterly synthesis of the creed. It declares that the Catholic Church has the power to forgive sins; it implies that on earth she alone has the power; it presupposes her uniqueness as the true Church of Christ, built by him on Peter, his Rock-Man and the Bearer of his Keys. Now, in his *Autobiography*, when Chesterton tries to explain what absolution does for the Catholic broken-hearted enough to receive it (as he was), and what motives of credibility it gives the non-Catholic open-minded enough to think about it (as he once had been), he says it restores a man to *childhood*, a strictly divine transformation of soul beyond the capacities of any merely human denomination. Emerging out of the confessional reminded him of entering into life, his own first early years in North Kensington, in which a 'strange daylight' seemed to shine on the 'steep roads down from Campden Hill, from which one could see the Crystal Palace from afar':

> Well, [he goes on to say] when a Catholic comes from Confession, he does truly, by definition, step out again into that dawn

[1.] *Autobiography*, London, Hutchinson, 1937, p. 329.

of his own beginning and look with new eyes across the world to a Crystal Palace that is really of crystal. He believes that in that dim corner, and in that brief ritual, God has really remade him in His own image. He is now a new experiment of the Creator. He is as much a new experiment as he was when he was really only five years old. He stands ... in the white light at the worthy beginning of the life of a man. The accumulations of time can no longer terrify. He may be grey and gouty, but he is only five minutes old.[2]

These words, inviting us to find his final end in his very beginning, are proof, so it seems to me, that spiritual childhood is not just one theme among many in Chesterton's thought, but rather the still point around which the whole Chestertonian universe turns. More importantly, chidlikeness is the chief quality of his soul, and therefore the first indication of his sanctity. What he thought and wrote, he lived. The goal of all his striving was to stay faithful to the child he used to be, or rather to live in the truth of that supernatural, baptismal childhood of which his and every man's natural childhood is the sign and promise. Conversion to the Catholic Church, and confession within her, were the God-given means confirming and bringing to completion Chesterton's lifelong resolve to heed the divine Saviour's words: 'Unless you be converted and become as little children, you shall not enter into the Kingdom of Heaven' (Mt 18: 3).

In what follows, I shall, first, define spiritual childhood with the help of St Thérèse of Lisieux, the Doctor of the Little Way, born just a year before Chesterton, canonised in his Catholic lifetime, the patron of the parish in which he died, the saint whom at first he found unappealing, but at the end, as he said in an unfinished letter from Lourdes, he had 'come to honour and understand better'.[3] Secondly, I shall show how Chesterton in his life and writings expounds and exemplifies spiritual childhood, especially by his child-like wonder at the world God has created, and his gratitude to the Creator for life, the primary and priceless gift of

---

[2.] Ibid., p. 329.

[3.] Maisie Ward, *Return to Chesterton*, London and New York, Sheed & Ward, 1952, p. 268.

sheer existence. Finally, I shall show how this wonder and gratitude, directed in trust and love towards God, fired Chesterton's lifelong struggle against the legitimating of suicide. As the culture of death that now surrounds us sets about legalising assisted suicide, Chesterton's wisdom and witness stand out as heroic, with the heroism proper to the charity and chivalry of a holy man. In his own time, and now again for ours, Chesterton is an apostle of the Gospel of Life.

The Little Way: The Obligatory Way

The Little Way of St Thérèse is not one possible path to Heaven, for, as she perceived so clearly, Christ our Lord made becoming a little child the condition of entry to the Kingdom, a commandment, not a counsel. Moreover, the Popes who raised Thérèse Martin to the honours of the altar, and appointed her the Church's thirty-third Doctor, have been faithful to the force of the divine Master's teaching. In 1997 Pope John Paul II said that his predecessors 'held up her holiness as an example for all'.[4] Note those words: *For all*. John Paul II said no more than Benedict XV ('In spiritual childhood is the secret of sanctity for *all the faithful* of the Catholic world')[5] or Pius XI ('We earnestly desire that *all the faithful* should study her in order to copy her, becoming children themselves, since otherwise they cannot, according to the words of the Master, arrive at the Kingdom of Heaven').[6] In St Thérèse we find a spirituality beyond the particularities of schools and charisms, the spirituality of the Gospel itself. This is the genius of the Little Flower, what makes her, in St Pius X's astonishing words, 'the greatest saint of modern times'.[7]

What, then, is spiritual childhood, the 'Little Way' of St Thérèse? First, and most broadly, it is a life lived, by the grace of the Holy Spirit, in the truth of one's baptism as a son-in-the-Son, an adopted child of God. Secondly, and

---

[4] *Divini amoris scientia* (1997), n. 3.
[5] 14 August 1921.
[6] 29 April 1923.
[7] Pope John Paul in *Divini amoris scientia*, n. 10.

more narrowly, it means, living that life by exercising the childlike virtues – humility, gratitude, and self-abandoning trust in Jesus and the Father – amidst the ordinary duties of daily existence.[8] Fourthly, spiritual childhood is a grace that flows from the Heart of the Infant and Crucified Word, a participation in his own self-emptying,[9] and it is communicated to us through the intercession and example of his Blessed Mother: Thérèse loves Mary, she tells us in her last poem, because she is the purest and most accessible example of the Little Way.[10] Finally, spiritual childlikeness is a supernatural protection against the psychological childishness to which fallen nature is prone: St Thérèse saw that the Little Way of self-abandonment to the heavenly Father required her to renounce the consolations of her childhood to which she was tempted to cling;[11] it was, in fact, the condition of spiritual maturity, the arming of her soul for combat with the powers of darkness. 'Out of the mouth of infants and of sucklings thou hast perfected praise, because of thy enemies, that thou mayest destroy the enemy and the avenger' (Ps 8: 3).

If the popes are right, and the mark of St Thérèse's greatness is the clarity of her perception, and the courage of her pursuit, of a path to holiness that all sorts and conditions

[8.] 'Jesus is pleased to show me the only way that leads to this divine furnace, this way that is the abandonment of the little child sleeping without fear in the arms of his father ... "Whosoever is a little one, let him come to me" (Prov. 9:4), as the Holy Spirit said by the lips of Solomon, and that same Spirit of Love has also said that "to them that are little, mercy is granted" (Wis. 6:7)' (MS B, p. 220, 1r).

[9.] The saint of Lisieux's devotion is equally to the Crib and the Cross: she is Thérèse of the Holy Child Jesus *and the Holy Face*.

[10.] 'You make me feel it's not impossible/ To follow in your footsteps, O Queen of the Elect,/ The narrow way to heaven you have made visible/ By always practising the humblest virtues,/ Close to you, Mary, I like to stay small,/ I see the vanity of worldly grandeur' ('Pourquoi je t'aime, ô Marie', *Oeuvres complètes*. Textes et dernières paroles, ed. Jacques Longchampt, Paris, Cerf, 1992, p. 751).

[11.] In the early hours of Christmas Day 1886 Thérèse was given what she called 'the grace of my complete conversion', which was at the same time 'the grace of leaving my childhood' (MS C 45r; *Oeuvres complètes*, p. 141).

of men can and indeed must follow if they want to reach their goal, then we should conclude that all the saints have, in some way, taken the Little Way. Consider, for example, what seems at first a most unlikely comparison with St Thérèse, namely, the Blessed John Henry Newman: what else but the Little Way is his 'Short Road to Perfection'? The Little Flower might have written the words herself: 'He … is perfect who does the work of the day perfectly, and we need not go beyond this to seek for perfection.'[12] What distinguishes St Thérèse from other saints, then, and what marks out Chesterton as man and writer, is not the practice of the Little Way, for, if our argument is valid, that practice is something they share with everyone who strives for Christian perfection. No, it is Thérèse Martin's and Gilbert Chesterton's explicit *understanding* of the Little Way, and their translation of that understanding into the way they exercise the Christian virtues, which singles them out among the great men and women of the Church in modern times.

Chesterton's Little Way

Chesterton would be the first to say that you can call him 'little' only by a most extravagant application of metaphor. Even so, however improbable it may seem when judged by tape measures and weighing scales, 'littleness', if we give it St Thérèse's theological interpretation, is without doubt the secret of GK's holiness; he proves to us that Christian magnanimity has childlike humility as its core and pre-condition.

The first evidence of Chesterton's spiritual childlikeness is to be observed in his relations with actual children. He and Frances had no family of their own, but he was godfather and 'unclet', as some of them called him, to a huge tribe of little ones, who later in life treasured the memory of not only his kindness and playfulness, but also what St Thomas Aquinas would have called his 'connatural'

[12.] John Henry Newman, *Meditations and Devotions*, new edn, New York, Longmans, Green & Co., 1907, p. 286.

understanding[13] of the mind of children: he could come close to them, in purity and without condescension, because he had preserved into manhood all that was best in his own childhood. Small children, he realised, apprehend reality in full sunlight, whereas greybeards tend to lose themselves in the fog of fads and fancies. As he said in some verses inscribed in the picture book he gave the child of one of his friends:

> Stand up and keep your childishness:
> Read all the pedants' screeds and strictures;
> But don't believe in anything
> That can't be told in coloured pictures.[14]

Much of the philosophy of St Thomas Aquinas, and indeed of St John Damascene's theology of the Incarnation and the holy icons, is in these few words dashed off at some birthday party in Beaconsfield. And what is so striking is not just the acuteness of insight, but the generosity of charity in thus instructing and encouraging the young.

The second proof of Chesterton's following of the Little Way is his humility, which, for the Church's Doctors, is the chief virtue signified by Our Lord in his teaching on becoming a little child. Ronald Knox, in the panegyric he preached at the Requiem in Westminster Cathedral, spoke of Gilbert's 'unbelievable humility', which, with his charity and chivalry, would remain with those who knew him 'as a more effective document of Catholic verity than any word even he wrote'.[15] The root of humility is the truth of our dependence on God in both nature and grace, of our nothingness as His creatures and our weakness as Adam's sons; but the essential act of humility is living willingly in accordance with that truth, refusing to show off our virtues and achievements, as if they had their exclusive source in ourselves, the readiness to be corrected by others and to learn from them, the resolve never to trample upon and humili-

---

[13.] *Summa theologiae* 2a2ae q. 45, a. 2.
[14.] Maisie Ward, *Return to Chesterton*, p. 88.
[15.] *Occasional Sermons of Ronald A. Knox*, ed. Philip Caraman SJ, London, Burns & Oates, 1960, p. 405.

ate those with whom one disagrees. Humility in all these aspects shines through almost every word Chesterton wrote and every action of his that is remembered. Self-mockery runs through his writings like a sparkling stream, and his generosity towards his intellectual foes is unrivalled in the public life of England. If proof be needed of Chesterton's heroic virtue, we need look no further than his incapacity to inspire enmity even in George Bernard Shaw and Herbert George Wells.

The third sign of Chesterton's 'little way' is his devotion to the littleness of God incarnate. If GKC is a theologian, then his theology has its centre in the Christmas mystery. Maisie Ward's words on this subject cannot be bettered:

> Some men, it may be, are best moved to reform by hate, but Chesterton was best moved by love, and nowhere does that love shine more clearly than in all he wrote about Christmas. It will be for this philosophy, this charity, this poetry that men will turn over the pages of *GK's Weekly* a century hence if the world still lasts.[16]

The Metaphysics of Wonder

From childhood to his last days, Chesterton felt wonder and gratitude at the world God has created. What absorbed and delighted him was not some other possible universe, but this actual universe in all its extraordinary ordinariness. Some visionaries may have imagined and sought a planet in which grass is purple, but Chesterton was astonished by the green grass of our own dear and familiar earth. Now, according to Plato and Aristotle, wonder is the beginning of philosophy: we feel wonder when an effect is manifest, but its cause obscure; and so we begin to dig and search, to look for the answer and the key to the door. If we are persistent in our wondering, we shall attain wisdom, be led finally to the highest cause of all, to God, the transcendent first cause of the universe. Such a man was Chesterton. Like

---

[16.] Maisie Ward, *Gilbert Keith Chesterton*, London, Sheed & Ward, 1944, p. 541.

St Augustine, he saw the fragile, contingent beauty of the things of this world as a message, a solemn proclamation: 'We did not make ourselves.'[17] And as the Bishop of Hippo did, the Journalist of Beaconsfield raised up his mind to the Maker of Heaven and earth.

One Thin Thread of Thanks

It was the memory of his childhood's amazement at existence, his insistence on being thankful for life, which delivered Chesterton from the spiritual darkness he endured in his youth. These were the early eighteen nineties, the naughty nineties, the nihilistic nineties, in which, in England as in France and Germany, men seemed intent on what Hans Urs von Balthasar has called 'the deification of death'.[18] The culture of death that now encompasses us was already well established among the intellectuals of the nineties: we see the same cult of perversity and sterility, though without today's flagrancy and political endorsement; the replacement of orthodox Christianity with the occult, or the worship of science, or a combination of the two; on all sides, as Paul Claudel said of his own France in this period, an 'aggressive and triumphant materialism and scepticism'.[19]

In the mental atmosphere of the nineties, human life comes to be regarded, not as a gift to be cherished, but as a commodity to be controlled, whether at its beginning or its end. The eugenicists are intent on breeding a master race, and on preventing the birth of those they deem unfit. H. G. Wells, writing in 1902, spits out his hatred for the 'gall-stones of vicious, helpless, and pauper masses', and insists that the 'swarms of black, and brown, and dirty-white, and yellow people, who do not come into the new needs of efficiency', will 'have to go'.[20] And from Nietzsche, now in his final years of madness in Germany, but all the rage in London as his works begin to appear in English, the

---

[17.] *Confessions*, lib. 11, cap. 4, n. 6.
[18.] The title of the third volume of his *Apokalpyse der deutschen Seele*, Salzburg, 1939.
[19.] *Oeuvres complètes*, vol. 28, Paris, 1978, p. 291f.
[20.] *Anticipations of the Reaction of Mechanical and Scientific Progress upon Human Life and Thought*, New York, 1902, pp. 87, 342.

intellectuals of the nineties learn the glorification of self-inflicted death, 'the free death', as Zaruthustra says, 'that comes to me because *I* will it'.[21]

Forty years later, in his *Autobiography*, Chesterton confesses the nightmares into which the pessimism of the nineties plunged him when he was a student at the Slade School of Art: 'I had an overpowering impulse to record or draw horrible ideas and images, plunging deeper and deeper as in a blind spiritual suicide.'[22]

Now, by the providence of God, he was saved through childhood, the reawakening of his own childhood's wonder and gratitude.

> When I had been for some time in these, the darkest depths of the contemporary pessimism, I had a strong inward impulse to revolt; to dislodge this incubus or throw off this nightmare. But as I was still thinking the thing out by myself, with little help from philosophy and no real help from religion, I invented a rudimentary and makeshift mystical theory of my own. It was substantially this: that even mere existence, reduced to its most primary limits, was extraordinary enough to be exciting. Anything was magnificent as compared with nothing. Even if the very daylight were a dream, it was a day-dream; it was not a nightmare ... I hung on to the remains of religion by one thin thread of thanks ... What I meant, whether or no I managed to say it, was this: that no man knows how much he is an optimist, even when he calls himself a pessimist, because he has not really measured the depths of his debt to whatever created him and enabled him to call himself anything. At the back of our brains, so to speak, there was a forgotten blaze or burst of astonishment at our own existence. The object of the artistic and spiritual life was to dig for this submerged sunrise of wonder, so that a man sitting in a chair might suddenly understand that he was actually alive, and be happy.[23]

[21.] 'Vom freien Tode', *Also sprach Zarathustra, Friedrich Nietzsche Werke*, vol. 2, ed. K. Schlechta, Munich, 1966, p. 334.

[22.] *Autobiography*, p. 93.

[23.] Ibid., pp. 94–5.

The Fundamental Fact of Being

These few lines of autobiography reveal Chesterton's natural affinity of mind with the metaphysics of St Thomas Aquinas, and the roots of his final adult reasonings in the first intuitions of his childhood. Chesterton holds what Aquinas holds: the proper object of the mind, the mind of the child and of every sane man, is *being*. As he puts it in his biography of St Thomas, the 'brilliant Victorian scientist' would like to think that the child looking out of the nursery window does not see the green lawn of the garden, but only a sort of 'green mist reflected in a tiny mirror of the human eye'. But St Thomas, in solidarity with the child and with Chesterton, 'says emphatically that the child is aware of *ens* [being]': 'Long before he knows that grass is grass, or self is self, he knows that something is something.'[24] Thus, says Chesterton, continuing the argument in his book on *Chaucer*, '[a]t the back of all our lives' there is this 'fundamental fact of being, as against not being', and 'he who has realized this reality knows that it does outweigh, literally to infinity, all lesser regrets or arguments for negation, and that under all our grumblings there is a subconscious substance of gratitude'.[25] In all of Chesterton's writing, this perception, overflowing into gratitude, of the marvel of sheer existence is conscious and explicit, and, after his conversion, and above all in his *Autobiography*, the gratitude is also for the grace of Catholic faith, for forgiveness through absolution, for supernatural life and childhood restored.

Suicide: The Sin of Sins

Nothing reveals more clearly Chesterton's spontaneous Thomism than what he says in *Orthodoxy* about suicide. These paragraphs of light and fire correspond closely to St Thomas's treatment of the same subject in the Second Part of the *Summa*. According to the Angelic Doctor, suicide is a sin against oneself, against one's neighbour, and against God. It is a sin against oneself, because the destruction of one's own

---

[24.] *St Thomas Aquinas*, new edn, London, Hodder & Stoughton, 1943, p. 133.
[25.] G. K. Chesterton, *Chaucer*, New York, 1932, p. 28.

life contradicts every created thing's natural in-clination to preserve itself in existence. But suicide is also a sin against one's fellow human beings. No man is an island; he is part of the continent, a limb of the body politic, the member of a community: his family, society at large, the human race. Now when he kills himself, a man cuts himself off from the common-wealth of man, diminishes it, and, of course, wounds its surviving individual members in a thousand ways. Suicide produces anguish in the friends and family of the self-mur-derer beyond any pain caused by, say, his physical or mental illness, or his moral disgrace. And when suicide does not cause anguish, when it is positively welcomed or officially tolerated by the community (as Lord Faulkner would like it to be), then it damages the social order even more deeply: by corrupting hearts and befouling minds.

Most gravely of all, suicide is a sin against God. No man can bring himself into existence, nor does he own himself: life is God's gift to man, and is subject to the power of him who, as Scripture says, 'kills and makes alive' (Deut 32:39). But to destroy what does not belong to you is gravely sinful, as is interfering in any serious matter that has not been entrusted to you. Therefore, suicide is in all circumstances gravely sinful.[26]

In *Orthodoxy*, without any apparent consultation of the actual text of St Thomas, Chesterton makes the arguments of St Thomas his own. The context is once again the nihilism of the nineties:

> Under the lengthening shadow of Ibsen, an argument arose whether it was not a very nice thing to murder one's self. Grave moderns told us that we must not even say 'poor fellow' of a man who had blown his brains out, since he was an enviable person, and had only blown them out because of their excep-tional excellence. Mr. William Archer [dramatic critic and the translator of Ibsen's *Ghosts*] even suggested that in the golden age there would be penny-in-the-slot machines by which a man could kill himself for a penny.[27]

26. *Summa theologiae* 2a2ae q. 64, a. 5.
27. G. K. Chesterton, *Orthodoxy*, new edn, London, Collins, 1961, p. 71.

Chesterton strikes his swordstick against this depravity, and in his own way articulates St Thomas's first argument, namely, that self-murder is the denial of that most fundamental inclination in man and all things, the longing for life and continuation in existence:

> In all this I found myself utterly hostile to many who called themselves liberal and humane. Not only is suicide a sin, it is *the* sin. It is the ultimate and absolute evil, the refusal to take an interest in existence; the refusal to take the oath of loyalty to life.[28]

Then, in the spirit of St Thomas, if not in literal dependence on him, Chesterton shows how the suicide, by wrenching himself out of existence, writes off the rest of the human race, and condemns in objective hatred every last part of the universe:

> The man who kills a man, kills a man. The man who kills himself, kills all men; as far as he is concerned he wipes out the world. His act is worse (symbolically considered) than any rape or dynamite outrage. For it destroys all buildings: it insults all women. The thief is satisfied with diamonds; but the suicide is not: that is his crime ... The thief compliments the things he steals, if not the owner of them. But the suicide insults everything on earth by not stealing it ... There is not a tiny creature in the cosmos at whom his death is not a sneer ... Of course there may be pathetic emotional excuses for the act. There often are for rape, and there almost always are for dynamite. But if it comes to clear ideas and the intelligent meaning of things, then there is much more rational and philosophic truth in the burial at the cross-roads and the stake driven through the body than in Mr Archer's suicidal automatic machines. There is a meaning in burying the suicide apart. The man's crime is different from other crimes – for it makes even crimes impossible.[29]

Here, argues Chesterton, is the essential difference between the suicide and the martyr. The martyr 'confesses this ultimate link with life; he sets his heart outside himself: he

[28.] Ibid., p. 71.
[29.] Ibid., pp. 71–2.

dies that something may live. The suicide is ignoble, because he has not this link with being: he is a mere destroyer; spiritually, he destroys the universe'.[30]

In *Orthodoxy*, Chesterton does not explicitly make St Thomas's third argument, suicide as a sin of injustice against the Creator to whom alone our lives belong, but in one of his Catholic books, *The Thing*, he comes close to it by showing how the man who kills himself sins against the good God by a perverse combination of presumption with despair, and a refusal to see nobility, even a mission and apostolate, in suffering bravely borne:

> A Catholic does not kill himself because he does not take it for granted that he will deserve Heaven in any case, or that it will not matter at all whether he deserves it at all. He does not profess to know exactly what danger he would run; but he does know what loyalty he would violate and what command or condition he would disregard. He actually thinks that a man might be fitter for Heaven because he endured like a man; and that a hero could be a martyr to cancer as St Lawrence or St Cecilia were martyrs to cauldrons or gridirons.[31]

We seem to have travelled a long distance from St Thérèse, but in fact only now have we caught up with her. Her finest hour, the final test of her childlike trust in God's merciful love, was the trial of faith she suffered in the last eighteen months of her life, when, with her body racked by consumption, her soul was tortured by temptations to doubt. Our Lord wanted His bride to take up a co-redemptive mission: to hear the voices of the nineties, of the decadents and the scientific atheists, to have a sense of their despair and their liability to suicide, to hear the voices and overcome them.[32] St Thérèse endured the darkness for the love of Christ, resisted it by his power, and thereby poured out on

---

30. Ibid., p. 72.
31. G. K. Chesterton, *The Thing*, London, Sheed & Ward, 1938, p. 222.
32. On one black day of pain, Thérèse confessed that 'if she had not had the faith, she would not have hesitated for a moment to put herself to death' (from the so-called *Cahiers verts*, 22 August 1897, *Oeuvres complètes*, p. 1104).

the wounded world of the nineties, and the even darker decades that followed them, the divine healing of him who is the Resurrection and the Life. Even in the struggle against suicide, Gilbert and Thérèse are one.

Conclusion

The autobiographies of holy people are not about themselves, or at least, though the subject matter is what they themselves said and did, the formal principle shaping the whole is what God did in them and for them. That is St Augustine's approach, as it is later St Teresa's and St Thérèse's. St Augustine's *Confessions* are a prayer addressed to God, and direct towards him the two acts denoted by the Latin verb, *Confiteor*, the acknowledgement of one's sin and the praise of God's goodness. Chesterton's *Autobiography* is in the same noble tradition. He speaks with grateful love of his parents and brother, of his wife and his friends, and of the wonders of the world as they were unfolded for him in his childhood, but of himself he says little except to parade his follies: the dunce at St Paul's and the lunatic at the Slade. The gags at his own expense begin in the book's second sentence.

Chesterton's *Autobiography* is his *Confessions*. Not only does it reach its conclusion with Peter, the Bearer of the Key, and his power to unlock Divine Mercy, it also gives hints in its earlier pages of a lifelong search for absolution. When he describes the morbidity of his youth, he says that, though he had not then heard of confession 'in any serious sense', that sacrament was, in fact, what he needed. Ten years later, confession was one of the subjects of his first conversation with Father O'Connor as they walked across the moors to Ilkley. O'Connor explained to Chesterton that, since 'there are only ten commandments and only three or four ways of breaking them', there is little excitement in hearing confessions, but that sometimes there is 'a rare thing among thrills: it is the vision of a submerged soul coming up out of the dark night of ocean into the pearly radiance of the morning'.[33] It was

---

[33.] John O'Connor, *Father Brown on Chesterton*, London, Burns, Oates & Washbourne, 1937, pp. 6–7.

this conversation about confession that inspired Chesterton's creation of Father Brown, in whom innocence of life coincides with a wisdom compounded of common sense, orthodox doctrine, and knowledge acquired in the confessional of the manifold weakness and wickedness of men.

In light of the *Autobiography* and the memories of his friends it should not surprise us to discover that it was the longing for divine forgiveness, and for the rejuvenating of his soul, that preoccupied Chesterton in the months leading up to his reception into the Church. As he said in a letter to Father Ronald Knox:

> I am concerned about what has become of a little boy whose father showed him a toy theatre, and a schoolboy whom nobody ever heard of, with his brooding on doubts and dirt and day-dreams of crude conscientiousness so inconsistent as to [be] near to hypocrisy, and all the morbid life of the lonely mind of a living person with whom I have lived. It is that story, that so often came near to ending badly, that I want to end well.[34]

And so it did. In a tin shack of a chapel in Beaconsfield, when Father O'Connor baptised him *sub conditione*, and heard his general confession, Chesterton's soul was resurrected ('My name is Lazarus, and I live'), and he was a child again, not in some fanciful psychological way, but in the firm ontological way affirmed by Catholic dogma: his sins blotted out by the Blood of Christ, and through the action of Christ's priest, his soul filled with the grace of the risen Christ, who alone can make the old man a new creation. Gilbert Keith Chesterton, aged forty-eight, was five minutes old, in a way more truly a child than 'the schoolboy whom nobody ever heard of'.

But in this story of confession and conversion, of childhood lost and regained, of a Catholic Englishman's 'unbelievable humility' and chivalry and charity, there is one detail – more than a detail, the jewel at its centre – which must not go unmentioned, and that is the part played in it by Our Lady, the Mother of the Little Way. Chesterton tells

[34.] Joseph Pearce, *Wisdom and Innocence: A Life of G. K. Chesterton*, San Francisco, Ignatius Press, 1996, p. 264.

us that he always saw the Church in Mary and Mary in the
Church, and that in moving towards the one he came closer
to the other.[35] Even in the dark days of the nineties, when
he was hardly even a Christian, the holy and lowly Virgin
gave him the hope that his childhood's sense of wonder and
gratitude was not unfounded, that it was in fact the key for
unlocking the universe. With these words of the boy Chesterton I shall end:

> The life that was Mary's shall guard us,
> > the dreams to high things that belong,
> The wonder, the holy, the highest shall stand
> > among men and be strong.[36]

---

[35] *The Well and the Shallows*; *The Collected Works of G. K. Chesterton*,
vol. 3, ed. George J. Marlin et al, San Francisco, Ignatius Press, 1990,
p. 463.

[36] 'Ave Maria', *The Debater*, February 1893; *The Collected Works of G. K.
Chesterton*, vol. 10, Collected Poetry, part 1, ed. Aidan Mackey, San
Francisco, Ignatius Press, 1994, p. 113.

Humour and Holiness in Chesterton

Ian Ker

The Chesterton jokes, of which the best known I suppose is the Market Harborough story, are familiar enough, but what his biographers, from Maisie Ward to Joseph Pearce, rather successfully hide is just how important humour was to Chesterton. First of all, of course, he was extremely funny both in life and in his writings, but, more than that, he saw life through the prism of humour, regarding comedy as a literary form that was certainly as important as tragedy. In this respect, he deplored what he saw as the modern refusal to turn 'a tragedy into a comedy' – even though 'almost all the primitive legends of the world are comedies'. The reader's 'sympathies', he insisted, 'are as much committed to the characters as if they were the predestined victims in a Greek tragedy'. And to speak about 'the artificiality of comedy', to say that it is 'in some sort of way superficial', was to betray 'a profound pessimism' about life, for the fact that this 'high and legitimate' form of art, 'glorified by Aristophanes and Molière', had 'sunk into such contempt' was 'due to the astonishing and ludicrous lack of belief in hope and hilarity which marks modern aesthetics'. So seriously did Chesterton take comedy that he saw it in quasi-religious terms: 'There is nothing to which a man must give himself with more faith and self-abandonment than to genuine laughter.' His favourite saint, Francis of Assisi, he wrote in another early essay, 'expressed in loftier and bolder language than any earthly thinker the conception that laughter is as divine as tears'.[1] Indeed, Chesterton thought, 'The comedy of man survives the tragedy of men.'[2]

This was not just theory: he was more than ready to put it into practice. It is revealing, for instance, that at about this time when he was engaged to Frances Blogg, he was composing love poems to her which are purely conventional and could have been written by any more or less accomplished versifier of the time, while, on the other hand, he was writing letters – *love* letters – such as only he could have written and which convey his feelings for her far more effectively *and* originally – through humour, admirably exemplifying his belief in the *seriousness* of humour that was to be such a prominent theme in his writings. Writing from the seaside, he attempts 'to reckon up the estate I have to offer you'. It included the 'admirable relic' of a straw hat, a walking stick 'admirably fitted to break the head of any denizen of Suffolk who denies that you are the noblest of ladies, but of no other manifest use', a copy of Whitman's poems, a packet of letters from a young lady, 'containing everything good and generous and loyal and wise that isn't in Whitman's poems', a pocket knife with a device to take stones out of a horse's hoof (given a horse with a lame foot, 'one stands prepared, with a defiant smile'), a 'Heart mislaid somewhere ...' As a reminder of his precarious financial situation, he included also 'about three pounds in gold and silver, the remains of [his employer] Mr. Unwin's bursts of affection: those explosions of spontaneous love for myself, which, such is the perfect order and harmony of his mind, occur at startlingly exact intervals of time'.

Humour was not only appropriate for conveying his love; it was also, startlingly, employed as a means of comforting his fiancée when her sister Gertrude, engaged to be married, was tragically killed in a road accident. He began

---

[1.] *Twelve Types*, London, Arthur L. Humphreys, 1902, p. 74, pp. 79–82; *The Defendant*, London, J. M. Dent, 1914, 123; *The Chesterton Review*, vol. xxvii, p. 292.

[2.] *G. K. Chesterton: The Collected Works*, San Francisco, Ignatius Press, 1986–, vol. XXVII, p. 121. All references are to this edition except where otherwise stated.

his first letter to Frances, who had gone to Italy to get over her bereavement:

> I am black but comely at this moment: because the cyclostyle has blacked me. Fear not. I shall wash myself. But I think it my duty to render an accurate account of my physical appearance every time I write: and shall be glad of any advice and assistance …

He refuses to apologise for his 'rambling levity': 'I have sworn that Gertrude should *not* feel, wherever she is, that the comedy has gone out of our theatre.'[3] Besides, his humour about his appearance, already a source of concern to his future wife, was deliberately intended to distract her from her grief.

The importance of humour is essential both for understanding Chesterton's concept of holiness and also for appreciating his own holiness. In his first novel, *The Napoleon of Notting Hill*, it is the humorist, 'who cares for nothing,' who 'possesses everything' – like the Pauline Christian who has nothing but possesses everything (2 Cor. 6:10). At the end we are told that the moral of the novel is that love and laughter should be inseparable.[4] The Christian God is a God of love, and man is created in his image. It is, therefore, highly significant for Chesterton that 'all animals except Man are serious',[5] that 'man is the only creature who does laugh':[6] 'Alone among the animals, he is shaken with the beautiful madness called laughter.'[7] The Christian God, then, must be a God of laughter if we are made in His image. And Chesterton concludes *Orthodoxy* by suggesting that:

[3.] Maisie Ward, *Gilbert Keith Chesterton*, London: Sheed and Ward, 1944, pp. 85–6, 97.

[4.] G. K. Chesterton, *Collected Works*, Vol. VI, pp. 274, 378.

[5.] G. K. Chesterton, *The Uses of Diversity: A Book of Essays*, London, Methuen, 1920, p. 1.

[6.] G. K. Chesterton, *Fancies Versus Fads*, London, Methuen, 1923, p. 122.

[7.] G. K. Chesterton, *The Everlasting Man*, San Francisco, Ignatius Press, 1993, p. 36.

There was something that He [Christ] hid from all men when He went up a mountain to pray. There was something that He covered instantly by abrupt silence or impetuous isolation. There was some one thing that was too great for God to show us when He walked upon our earth; and I have sometimes fancied that it was His mirth.[8]

He was more explicit in his verse. A poem called 'Secrecy' begins, 'Laughter is sacred', and ends:

> But mirth is sacred: when from all his own
> He sundered, going up a mount to pray
> Under the terrible stars in stern array
> Upon the lonely peak he laughed aloud.

In a poem called 'The Fish', he 'knew there can be laughter/ On the secret face of God'.[9]

Humour, then, Chesterton saw as integral to Christianity – or rather to Catholic Christianity. But it was possible to be a Catholic in spirit if not in letter. This was true of his beloved Dickens, who understood that, 'A good joke is the one ultimate and sacred thing.'[10] But while Dickens was in Chesterton's eyes an essentially medieval, and therefore Catholic writer,[11] he complained that

> There was a complete absence from modern, popular supernaturalism of the old popular mirth. We hear plenty to-day of the wisdom of the spiritual world; but we do not hear, as our fathers did, of the folly of the spiritual world, of the tricks of the gods, and the jokes of the patron saints.

It was the chief reason why Dickens, who was 'immoderately possessed' with humour, was such an important writer for Chesterton. Dickens understood only too well that

---

[8.] G. K. Chesterton, *Orthodoxy*, London, Hodder & Stoughton, 1908, pp. 365–6.

[9.] G. K. Chesterton, *Collected Works*, Vol. X, pt. 1, pp. 167, 212.

[10.] Ibid., Vol. XV, p. 253.

[11.] I have developed this point in *The Catholic Revival in English Literature, 1845–1961*, Notre Dame, In., University of Notre Dame Press, 2003, pp. 76, 79–80, 82–9.

Exhilaration is not a physical accident but, but a mystical fact; that exhilaration can be infinite, like sorrow; that a joke can be so big that it breaks the roof of the stars. By simply going on being absurd, a thing can become godlike; there is but one step from the ridiculous to the sublime.[12]

George Bernard Shaw, on the other hand, was fatally flawed in Chesterton's eyes by being over-serious, in the bad sense of solemn: he was 'too serious to enjoy Shakespeare', for instance, lacking that Elizabethan 'exuberance', with which Dickens also was so well endowed, that made the Elizabethan writers 'so exuberant and exultant in their mere joy of existence that their mirth is not even obvious, and not even facetious. These gods are shaken with a mysterious laughter. They seem torn by the agony of jokes as incommunicable as the wisdom of the gods'. Unlike the Puritan Shaw, Shakespeare had the 'quality' of 'the comic supernatural', of the idea of 'energies in the universe being actually merrier than we'. Shaw was 'never frivolous', 'never irresponsible even for an instant'. He was witty, certainly, but his wit was 'never a weakness'; consequently it was 'never a sense of humour'. Wit, insists Chesterton, which 'is always connected with the idea that truth is close and clear', is quite distinct from humour, which 'is always connected with the idea that truth is tricky and mystical and easily mistaken'. Thus Shaw 'never said an indefensible thing; that is, he never said a thing that he was not prepared brilliantly to defend'. For he was 'a great wit' but he was no humorist. And here Chesterton makes the distinction between wit and humour a religious distinction:

> Humour is akin to agnosticism, which is only the negative side of mysticism. But pure wit is akin to Puritanism; to the perfect and painful consciousness of the final fact in the universe. Very briefly, the man who sees the consistency in things is a wit – and a Calvinist. The man who sees the inconsistency in things is a humorist – and a Catholic.[13]

It was the Puritans who had destroyed Catholic mediaeval

---

12. G. K. Chesterton, *Collected Works*, Vol. XV, p. 50.
13. Ibid., Vol. XI, pp. 347–8, 357–8, 380–1.

'Merrie England', with its 'union of mystery with farce' and its 'merry supernaturalism'.[14] It was impossible for a Puritan to be frivolous: 'A frivolous Puritan was not a Puritan at all.' But 'a frivolous Catholic' was by no means a contradiction in terms. Outsiders, who could not see their internal faith, were puzzled by Catholics' external 'frivolity'. Thomas More 'actually died laughing' and 'joking'.[15]

As I have already indicated, humour for Chesterton was an entirely serious thing. The humorous was not opposed to the serious but to the solemn. 'About what other subjects can one make jokes,' he had once asked, 'except serious subjects?' 'Funny' was not 'the opposite of serious' but 'the opposite of not funny'. After all, in the Bible there were 'any number of ... jokes'. In the Book of Job, the book which interested Chesterton so much, God himself, who is depicted 'easily and carelessly' as 'laughing and winking', 'overwhelms Job with a torrent of levities'. Even 'a careless joke', Chesterton argued, was not 'fundamentally and really frivolous': 'The thing which is fundamentally and really frivolous is a careless solemnity.'[16] To say that one must not 'joke about sacred subjects' is to say that one 'must not jest at all', for 'there are no subjects that are not sacred subjects. Every instant of human life is awful.' And the truth is that 'Life is too uniformly serious not to be joked about.' But because life is so 'serious' it did not mean that 'living' life had to be 'serious all the time'. It was all right to be solemn about 'frivolous' things but not about serious things: 'You can be a great deal too solemn about Christianity to be a good Christian.' The alternative to not having 'mirth' about the really serious things like religion was 'madness'.[17] It was not honesty but hypocrisy that was 'solemn': 'Honesty always laughs, because things are so laughable.'[18] Jokes,

14. G. K. Chesterton, *The Common Man*, London, Sheed and Ward, 1950, p. 20.
15. G. K. Chesterton, *Collected Works*, Vol. XVIII, pp. 371–2.
16. Ibid., Vol. I, pp. 157, 159–61.
17. G. K. Chesterton, *Lunacy and Letters*, ed. Dorothy Collins, London and New York, Sheed and Ward, 1958, pp. 95–7.
18. G. K. Chesterton, *The Apostles and the Wild Ducks and other essays*, ed. Dorothy Collins, London, Paul Elek, 1975, p. 136.

he thought, were 'generally honest', whereas 'Complete solemnity is almost always dishonest.'[19] To take 'everything seriously' is to make 'an idol of everything'.[20] Chesterton enjoys teasing his readers with the paradox that it is 'so easy to be solemn' but 'so hard to be frivolous'.[21]

A humourless Christianity was for Chesterton a defective Christianity. Because it was a 'universal' religion it was both a 'serious' religion but also because 'universal ... full of comic things': 'It is the test of a responsible religion ... whether it can take examples from pots and pans and boots and butter-tubs. ... It is the test of a good religion whether you can joke about it.'[22] And that for Chesterton included joking vulgarly about it:

> When once you have got hold of a vulgar joke, you may be certain that you have got hold of a subtle and spiritual idea. The men who made the joke saw something deep which they could not express except by something silly and emphatic.

The commonest of vulgar jokes were 'really theological jokes' being 'concerned with the Dual Nature of Man. They refer to the primary paradox that man is superior to all the things around him and yet is at their mercy'.[23] Anyway Chesterton thought that a joke was 'always a thought; it is grave and formal writing that can be quite literally thoughtless'.[24]

Chesterton was profoundly convinced that to be serious is to be humorous and that where humour is missing it is not seriousness that one encounters but solemnity, which is flippant in the deepest sense. There is a delightfully funny letter he wrote to a young Catholic friend of his, Clare Nicholl, whose family had become close friends with the Chestertons in their later years, which beautifully makes the point. The letter is quoted by Maisie Ward in her supplement to her biography, *Return to Chesterton* – but it is

[19.] G. K. Chesterton, *Collected Works*, Vol. XXVII, p. 95.
[20.] G. K. Chesterton, *The Uses of Diversity*, p. 1.
[21.] G. K. Chesterton, *All Things Considered*, London, Methuen, 1908, p. 2.
[22.] G. K. Chesterton, *Collected Works*, Vol. XXVII, pp. 205–6.
[23.] Ibid., Vol. XXVIII, pp. 66–7.
[24.] G. K. Chesterton, *The Uses of Diversity*, p. 72.

characteristically ignored by the subsequent (humourless, it must be said) biographers. Chesterton is writing from California where he was on his second American lecture tour of 1930–1. Frances was with him, convalescing from a flu virus she had picked up in Tennessee. As 'an exile', Chesterton tells Clare, he has learned 'to hate time': 'I see a new and savage sense in the figure of Killing Time. I handle the large knife in my pocket.' He intends, at any rate, to 'dramatise' for her benefit'

> a real scene, farce, comedy or miracle play: which occurred in Chattanooga in the State of Tennessee (which is Puritan and very Dry), near Dayton of the Monkey Trial. Frances in bed. To her enters a perfectly gigantic Popish Priest, swarthy as a Spaniard but bearing the reassuring name of [it was an Irish name].
>
> *Priest* (after a boisterous greeting) I was told ye were ill: but I didn't know how ill. I've brought the Holy Oils.
>
> *Frances* (somewhat tartly) Then you can take 'em away again. I don't want *them* just yet. But I wish you'd give me your blessing, Father.
>
> *Priest* I'll give ye some whiskey first.
>
> (Produces an enormous bottle of Bootleg Whiskey and flourishes it like a club). Don't ye believe all that yer told about the stuff we get – you've only got to know your Bootlegger. This is perfectly sound mellow Canadian stuff and the nurse says ye need a little stimulant.
> (Administers a little stimulant with a convivial air.)
> You drink that down and ye'll be all the better.
>
> *Frances* (rather faintly) … and the Blessing?
>
> *Priest* (straightens himself and gabbles in a strong guttural voice) *Benedicat te Omnipotens Deus*, etc., or whatever is the form for sickbeds.
>
> **Curtain**

Now one might think that Chesterton is just sending an amusing letter to his young friend, but actually the fun carries a serious intention: he wants to make an important point to Clare about her religion.

> I should like to have that actual dialogue printed as a little Catholic leaflet and circulated by the C.T.S. [Catholic Truth Society]. It would tell people more about the Soul of the Church than ten thousand chippy chats between A (Anglican Enquirer) and C (Catholic Instructor) – about its fearlessness of the facts of life and the Fact of Death, its ease and healthy conscience, its contempt for fads and false laws, its buoyancy that comes from balance: its naturalness with the natural body as with the supernatural soul: its freedom from sniffing and snuffling embarrassment: its utter absence of the Parson ...

Chesterton is being utterly serious: he really does believe that comic dialogue is a more powerful apologetic for the Catholic Church than any amount of more formal theological apologetics. And he does not hesitate to draw the moral for his young friend:

> Clare dear, never let go of the Faith. At unlucky moments, in unworthy people, it may sometimes turn on us a face that is harsh or features that are irritant: but in moments like that, when Reality is only too close, you suddenly see it quite plain: the face of your best friend: and in the sick-room that wind from beyond the world is only something fresher than fresh air.[25]

Why was humour so important to Chesterton and why did he think it such a significant note of Catholic Christianity? First and most important, like any orthodox Christian, he believed, to use his own words, that 'the most deadly moral danger' is 'the danger of egoism and spiritual pride'.[26] The opposite of pride is, of course, humility, the one virtue unknown to pagans:

[25] Maisie Ward, *Return to Chesterton*, London and New York, Sheed & Ward, 1952, pp. 247–8.

[26] G. K. Chesterton, *Come to Think of it*, London, Methuen, 1930, p. 121.

The greatest of Christian doctors were the first to admit that most of the Christian virtues had been heathen virtues. They only claimed that Christianity could alone really inspire a heathen to observe the heathen virtues.

Humility was the one exception: 'Upon one point and one point only, was there really a moral revolution that broke the back of human history. And that was upon the point of Humility.' This, 'the greatest psychological discovery that man has made, since man has sought to know himself,' was 'the stupendous truth that man does not know anything, until he can not only know himself but ignore himself'.

Pride, writes Chesterton, is 'the falsification of fact, by the introduction of self' and is 'the enduring blunder of mankind': 'Christianity would be justified if it had done nothing but begin by detecting that blunder.'[27] Chesterton's point is that humility is not simply a moral virtue but also essential for knowledge: 'The truth is, that all genuine appreciation rests on a certain mystery of humility ...'[28] In one of his early essays he wrote: 'Whatever virtues a triumphant egoism really leads to, no one can reasonably pretend that it leads to knowledge.' It is only the humble, he says, who can see 'the towering and tropical vision of things as they really are'. In the same essay he claims that, because humility 'has been discredited as a virtue at the present day', 'joy' has been replaced by 'the bitterness of Greek pessimism' which has been revived by 'the splendour of Greek self-assertion'.[29] But splendid as that self-assertion may be, it has nothing like the power of Christian humility, which 'is not only the strongest thing in the world, but the most for-midable and even the fiercest thing in the world'.[30] That makes humility sound a somewhat austere, even humourless kind of thing. But that is very far indeed from Chesterton's conception of humility, which for him is very closely bound up with humour.

[27.] G. K. Chesterton, *Collected Works*, Vol. V, pp. 655–6.
[28.] Ibid., Vol. I, p. 69.
[29.] *The Defendant*, London, J. M. Dent, 1914, pp. 133–4, 137.
[30.] G. K. Chesterton, *Collected Works*, Vol. XXVII, p. 392.

Writing in his early book *Heretics* on Whistler, he suggests that because of his colossal vanity the painter 'never laughed at all. There was no laughter in his nature; because there was no thoughtlessness and self-abandonment, no humility'.[31] And where there is no laughter there is no joy either – 'no strong sense of an unuttered joy' without 'a hearty laugh'.[32] Humility and laughter are so interconnected that without humility there can be no humour, as in the case of Whistler, but equally without humour there can be no humility: 'Humour is meant, in a literal sense, to make game of man; that is, to dethrone him from his official dignity and hunt him like game.' Yes, admits Chesterton, 'Joking is undignified; that is why it is good for one's soul. Do not fancy you can be a detached wit and avoid being a buffoon; you cannot. If you are the Court Jester you must be the Court Fool.'[33] It is not just a question of other people laughing at one; one has to be able to laugh at oneself before laughing at anything else: 'No man has ever laughed at anything till he has laughed at himself.'[34]

Chesterton thought that 'of all the iron elements in the eternal soul none is more fixed or more enduring than its frivolity', that 'ancient laughter', that 'elemental agony, shaking the jester himself' which is the great enemy of pride, for to be 'mirthful' is to abandon 'dignity, which is another name for spiritual pride': 'A laugh is like a love affair in that it carries a man completely off his feet; a laugh is like a creed or a church in that it asks that a man should trust himself to it.' Like St Francis, whose 'sense of humour ... prevented him from ever hardening into the solemnity of sectarian self-righteousness',[35] Chesterton believes in the divinity of laughter:

A man must sacrifice himself to the God of Laughter, who has stricken him with a sacred madness. As a woman can make a

[31.] Ibid., Vol. I, p. 170.
[32.] Ibid., pp. 151–2.
[33.] G. K. Chesterton, *Alarms and Discursions*, London, Methuen, 1910, pp. 200–1.
[34.] G. K. Chesterton, *Collected Works*, Vol. XXIX, p. 546.
[35.] Ibid., I, p. 131.

fool of a man, so a joke makes a fool of a man. And a man must love a joke more than himself, or he will not surrender his pride for it.[36]

A laugh for Chesterton is greatly superior to a smile: 'Laughter has something in it in common with the ancient winds of faith and inspiration; it unfreezes pride ... it makes men forget themselves in the presence of something greater than themselves ...'[37] In short, it is the 'chief antidote to pride'.[38] Not surprisingly, the philanthropists so hated by Chesterton were lacking in 'two things' – 'laughter and humility'.[39]

By virtue of their poverty the poor are of necessity humble, and naturally Chesterton sees this humility as accompanied by humour. The 'tragedy' of London, 'the largest of the bloated modern cities ... the smokiest ... the dirtiest ... the most sombre ... the most miserable', is matched by its 'comedy' and 'farce', being certainly 'the most amusing and the most amused' of modern cities, for 'the great boast' of England – 'perhaps the greatest boast that is possible to human nature' – is that 'the most unhappy part of our population is also the most hilarious part'.[40] The poor of London were notable for their 'persistent tragedy' but also for their 'persistent farce and their persistent frivolity'.[41]

True, humour was the 'one grand quality' of the English, but the 'most tragic part of our population is also the most comic part': 'The slums exist in one incessant state of satire ... Irony is the very atmosphere of the poor.'[42] The 'common people' of England were 'starved of both religion

---

36. G. K. Chesterton, *A Handful of Authors: Essays on Books and Writers*, ed. Dorothy Collins, London and New York, Sheed and Ward, 1953, pp. 28–9.
37. G. K. Chesterton, *The Common Man*, p. 158.
38. G. K. Chesterton, *The Spice of Life and other Essays*, ed. Dorothy Collins, Beaconsfield, Darwen Finlayson, 1964, p. 29.
39. G. K. Chesterton, *Collected Works*, Vol. XXVII, p. 360.
40. G. K. Chesterton, *All Things Considered*, pp. 11–12.
41. G. K. Chesterton, *Lunacy and Letters*, 116.
42. G. K. Chesterton, *Collected Works*, Vol. XXVII, p. 389; *A Handful of Authors*, p. 49.

and democracy', but they 'lived' on 'laughter', their 'sub-
stitute for religion, for property, and sometimes even for
food'.[43] And Chesterton considered 'the humour of an
omnibus conductor or a railway porter' to be 'a much more
powerful and real thing than most modern forms of education and eloquence'.[44] But although he associated humour
particularly with England's poor, he believed that this 'very
Christian thing', 'the great national heritage of humour',
was the 'great national contribution to the culture of
Christendom'.[45]

Humour is a 'very Christian thing' if only because man is
made in the image of God, the Christian God of laughter,
and it is laughter, according to Chesterton, that is 'the
instinct which guards human dignity'; 'barbarians', on the
other hand, 'exhibit a lack of laughter almost like that of the
beasts that perish.'[46] The modern 'serious sexual novel', for
example – Chesterton is presumably thinking above all of
D. H. Lawrence – crushes and silences 'laughter like an evil
passion', sacrificing 'the noble and ancestral gift of laughter,
... the power of uproarious reaction against ourselves and
our own incongruities'.[47] Laughter for Chesterton is a spiritual weapon, which effects the 'enlargement of the soul'.[48]
And just as the soul may be 'rapt out of the body in an agony
of sorrow, or a trance of ecstasy', so too it may be 'rapt out of
the body in a paroxysm of laughter'.[49] A comic character like
Bottom in *A Midsummer Night's Dream* has 'the supreme
mark of ... real greatness in that like the true saint ... he only
differs from humanity in being as it were more human than
humanity'.[50]

It is time again to turn from Chesterton's theory to his
practice. I have only found two criticisms of his character

[43.] G. K. Chesterton, *Collected Works*, Vol. XXX, p. 536.
[44.] Ibid., Vol. XVI, p. 124.
[45.] Ibid., Vol. XVIII, pp. 245, 309–10.
[46.] Ibid., Vol. XXX, p. 292.
[47.] Ibid., Vol. XXXII, p. 444.
[48.] Ibid., Vol. XXXI, p. 112.
[49.] G. K. Chesterton, *The Common Man*, p. 12.
[50.] Ibid., p. 17.

that were made by contemporaries. First and least important, an occasional flash of irritability was noticed – surely a fault few of us can be entirely free of. Thus his great friend Fr John O'Connor on one occasion was startled when late one evening after a party at the studio that would be enlarged to become 'Top Meadow', he offered his arm to Chesterton who 'refused it with a finality foreign to our friendship'.[51] The truth is that, although, or perhaps because, Chesterton frequently made jokes about his size, he was self-conscious about it. But the important point to notice about this little episode was how startled O'Connor was: it was simply quite inconsistent with Chesterton's usual imperturbable good humour. Similarly, Clare Nicholl remembered how one evening at supper Chesterton asked her if she would like red or white wine, to which she replied that she was happy with either if Frances was also having some.

> To my dismay G. K. slapped the bottle he was holding onto the table, positively glared at me and said forcefully, 'Look here, Clare, if you want wine, say so: if you don't want wine, say so: but for goodness' sake *don't* make your having wine or not having wine dependent on what other people do.'

But Clare also remembered how angered he would be by unkindness or 'uncharitable gossip', although he 'very rarely found fault openly, but the offender would know by his silence and sudden lack of response'.[52]

More serious was the criticism of a certain selfishness that observers thought they discerned in Chesterton. Robert Blatchford, with whom Chesterton engaged in a lengthy controversy, recalled 'with contempt an occasion when he went out into the rain to get a cab for his wife, while Frances went out into the rain to get a cab for her husband'.[53] But one has to remember that until his marriage Chesterton had lived at home with his parents, where he was accustomed to his mother doing everything practical for him. Frances

---

[51.] John O'Connor, *Father Brown on Chesterton*, London, Burns, Oates & Washbourne, 1938, pp. 78–9.

[52.] Maisie Ward, *Return to Chesterton*, pp. 196–7.

[53.] Ibid., p. 80.

simply took over where his mother left off. She could get impatient with her hopelessly impractical husband, as their hostess at South Bend on their second American trip remembered.[54] But there is no record of her ever seriously complaining: this was their marital arrangement and by all accounts they were an extremely happy couple. Besides, as a woman, Frances had no children of her own to mother – only her husband. A more serious criticism came from Freda Spencer, one of Chesterton's secretaries.

Asked for her memories, she told Maisie Ward, first, that she marvelled at how her employer 'could have spent so much time and talent merely for the sake of giving pleasure and amusement to entirely unimportant people ... He gave to the trivialities of life a richness and importance which was essentially Christian', providing 'fun and laughter which enlivened the daily round'. But she found this total unselfishness inconsistent with an odd kind of selfishness.

> What I always did find hard to appreciate in him, and I, personally, think it spoilt him and made life very difficult for those who had to do with him, was his utter abhorrence of anything approaching discipline, restraint, or order. He could not tolerate the suggestion of such things being applied to life at all, and, carried to extremes, it is an irritating and exhausting attitude for those who have to cope with it. I think this attitude of his put a great strain on Mrs. Chesterton, who had the whole responsibility of his well-being, the household, the finances and at one time, at any rate, of his work, on her shoulders. He could get as nearly angry as I should think it was possible for him to be, if he detected her in any attempt to bring order or discipline into his or indeed anyone else's life.[55]

Freda Spencer was no doubt unaware of the cause of this strange penchant for anarchy, which lay in the unusually undisciplined upbringing that Chesterton and his brother had enjoyed, in which, for example, their parents would allow them to argue for hours uninterruptedly and regardless of meals.

---

54. Ibid., p. 253.
55. Ibid., pp. 156–7.

Now in considering whether somebody should be raised to the altars the Catholic Church is not looking for flawlessness but for heroic virtue. And I think that all Chesterton's contemporaries would have agreed with the suitably paradoxical proposition that he practised what may look like something of an oxymoron, the quality of *heroic humility*. In his panegyric at his funeral Mass in Westminster Cathedral, Ronald Knox singled out his 'unbelievable humility' as 'a more effective document of Catholic verity than any word even he wrote'.[56] Contemporaries never doubted the absolute sincerity of his modesty about his writings, a most unusual quality in a writer. Clare Nicholl, to give just one example of the many examples one could give, remembered his 'genuinely surprised' reaction to her request to borrow a new novel he had just published – 'My dear girl, if you really want to read it …'[57] There was nothing of Uriah Heep in Chesterton's humility: it was a very attractive humility, shot through as it was with *humour*.

I mentioned at the beginning of this essay that it surprises me how reticent, apart from retelling the familiar stories, his biographers have been not only about how funny Chesterton was but also about the importance he attached to humour, of which we can find a virtual philosophy or rather theology in his writings. In connection with this reticence, it also surprises me how very little attention his biographers have paid to his *Autobiography*, a work which I think can be placed alongside such classic autobiographies as Newman's *Apologia pro Vita sua* and Ruskin's *Praeterita*. One would not, of course, go to the *Autobiography* for dates or for factual and chronological accuracy (one would not go to any of Chesterton's books for such things), but the book is immensely significant for the self-portrait that its author draws, in particular for the humorous self-deprecation that runs through its delightful pages.

I would like to conclude by citing two passages in the book. The first tells three jokes against Chesterton himself:

My last American tour consisted of inflicting no less than

[56.] *GK's Weekly*, 2 July 1936.
[57.] Maisie Ward, *Return to Chesterton*, p. 198.

ninety-nine lectures on people who never did me any harm;
and ... the adventure, which was very enjoyable, breaks up like
a dream into isolated incidents. An aged Negro porter, with
a face like a walnut, whom I discouraged from brushing my
hat, and who rebuked me saying, 'Ho, young man. Yo's losing
yo dignity before yo time. Yo's got to look nice for de girls.' A
grave messenger who came to me in a Los Angeles hotel, from
a leading film magnate, wishing to arrange for my being pho-
tographed with the Twenty-Four Bathing-Beauties; Leviathan
among the Nereids; an offer which was declined amid general
surprise.[58]

It strikes me as remarkable how little attention is paid by
those who write about Chesterton – as a glance through the
back numbers of *The Chesterton Review* soon reveals – to
marvellous passages like this, and indeed to the *Autobiography* itself. In fact, I can only suppose that the biographers
and critics of Chesterton do indeed share in that contempt
for comedy that Chesterton so deplored, as I pointed out at
the beginning of this essay.

The other, longer passage I want to quote is, in my view,
one of the two funniest passages in an autobiography, rich
in self-deprecating humour. It describes an incident early
on in Chesterton's career and occurs, with typical disregard
for any kind of chronological order, in the last chapter. I
need hardly say it is not quoted or even referred to in any of
the biographies.

In those early days, especially just before and just after I was
married, it was my fate to wander over many parts of England,
delivering what were politely called lectures. There is a considerable appetite for such bleak entertainments, especially
in the north of England, the south of Scotland and among
certain active Nonconformist centres even in the suburbs of
London. With the mention of bleakness there comes back to
me the memory of one particular chapel, lying in the last fea-
tureless wastes to the north of London, to which I actually
had to make my way through a blinding snow-storm, which I
enjoyed very much; because I like snowstorms. In fact, I like
practically all kinds of English weather except that particular

58. G. K. Chesterton, *Collected Works*, Vol. XVI, p. 300.

sort of weather that is called 'a glorious day'. So none need
weep prematurely over my experience, or imagine that I am
pitying myself or asking for pity. Still, it is the fact that I was
exposed to the elements for nearly two hours either on foot or
on top of a forlorn omnibus wandering in a wilderness; and by
the time I arrived at the chapel I must have roughly resembled
the Snow Man that children make in the garden. I proceeded
to lecture, God knows on what, and was about to resume
my wintry journey, when the worthy minister of the chapel,
robustly rubbing his hands and slapping his chest and beaming
at me with the rich hospitality of Father Christmas, said in a
deep, hearty, fruity voice, 'Come, Mr. Chesterton; it's a bitter
cold night! Do let me offer you an Oswego biscuit.' I assured
him gratefully that I felt no such craving; it was very kind of
him, for there was no possible reason, in the circumstances for
his offering me any refreshment at all. But I confess that the
thought of returning through the snow and the freezing blast,
for two more hours, with the glow of that one biscuit within
me, and the Oswego fire running through all my veins, struck
me as a little out of proportion. I fear it was with considerable
pleasure that I crossed the road and entered a public-house
immediately opposite the chapel, under the very eyes of the
Nonconformist Conscience.[59]

Now this glorious passage is far funnier than any passage
that I can find in Chesterton's novels, even though it would
make a most amusing scene in a novel: for it is remarkable
how lacking in comedy and humour the fiction is, compared
for instance to the *Autobiography*, proving, as in other
respects, Chesterton's point that he was not 'a real novelist'
though he *was* a real journalist[60] – although an exception
has to be made for the innovative and original *The Man who
was Thursday*. Much has been written on the novels including a full-length book. But if anyone can point to a book
or even article where this passage from the *Autobiography*
is quoted or even referred to, I shall be very pleasantly
astonished.

[59.] G. K. Chesterton, *Collected Works*, Vol. XVI, pp. 314–5.
[60.] Ibid., Vol. XVI, pp. 276–7.

The Christian as Doctor of the Church: The Case of G. K. Chesterton

Aidan Nichols

Introduction

Any attempt to present Chesterton as the very model of a modern Catholic Christian is required to come to terms with the question of his orthodoxy. When the Church recognises in someone the qualities that make up a saint, she seeks to know about their mind as well as their heart, for the very good biblical reason that in the religion of the Gospel what is carried out in ethics, by virtuous living, is, in the words of the apostle, *the truth*. Christian discipleship is 'doing the truth in love', or, in a more literal translation of the Letter to the Ephesians, 'truthing in love', *alêtheuontes de en agapê*.[1] In Christianity, the splendour of the truth is what commands morals, and this will be, then, not just moral truth narrowly conceived but the truth of the God-man and his Spirit who enter the world of our space and time as the 'two hands' – thus St Irenaeus – of the Father's charity, with a view to changing our existence. Gospel conversion requires transformed minds as well as hearts. Divine revelation changes our minds, our intellectual outlook, as well as our hearts, our loves and our feelings. Saints needs supernatural

---

[1.] Ephesians 4:15. The classic English Catholic translation comes via the Vulgate: *veritatem autem facientes in charitate*.

intelligence as well as supernaturalised wills and emotions. In his 2009 encyclical *Caritas in veritate*, Pope Benedict XVI observes:[2] 'Only in truth does charity shine forth, only in truth can charity be authentically lived. Truth is the light that gives meaning and value to charity'. A fortiori is this true when the saints we are speaking of are Doctors of the Church. Indeed, orthodoxy is as vital to being recognised as a doctor as is holiness of life.

When in 2007 I used the last phase of a short term lecture-ship in the University of Oxford to look into the question of Chesterton's theological doctrine as found in the writings of his Anglo-Catholic and Roman Catholic periods, I found no reason to fault him on this score – which, perhaps, as the author of a two-volume study guide to the *Catechism of the Catholic Church* I was in a position to do.[3] Indeed, I found Chesterton's presentation of doctrine inspirational – which is what one would expect from a theologian who may well be a doctor as distinct from a plodder such as myself. The materials I put together covered a large range of subject matter: Chesterton's apologetics or fundamental theology, his account of God's existence, his theological doctrine of man, his Christology and soteriology, his theology of history, his theological ethics, his ecclesiology and (albeit briefly) his eschatology. To condense even the most impor-tant points and texts from a course's worth of lectures – subsequently a book[4] – is scarcely practicable in an essay of this length. So instead I propose to exploit a useful ambiguity in the title given to me by the editor of this col-lection.

A 'doctor of the Church' can mean one of two things. First, and more usually, it means a writer or possibly

2. Benedict XVI, *Caritas in veritate* 2.

3. A. Nichols, OP, *The Splendour of Doctrine. The* Catechism of the Cath-olic Church *on Christian Believing*, Edinburgh, T. & T. Clark, 1995; idem., *The Service of Glory. The* Catechism of the Catholic Church *on Worship, Ethics, Spirituality*, Edinburgh, T. & T. Clark, 1997.

4. Idem., *G. K. Chesterton, Theologian*, Manchester, NH, Sophia Institute Press and London, Darton, Longman and Todd, 2009. I am grateful to these publishers for permission to reproduce here some of the material offered there.

preacher whom the Church has acknowledged as the distinctive kind of saint who is a teacher of the faith par excellence. But the phrase 'doctor of the Church' could also mean, secondly, and less commonly, one such teacher who has made a special contribution to, in particular, the theme of the Church: her mystery and her life. Just so we speak, for instance, of St Augustine as 'the doctor of grace', meaning to indicate how the Bishop of Hippo made a notable contribution to understanding the topic of grace: divine goodness energising in us to liberate our wills from within. So my contribution focuses on Chesterton, the theologian of the Church. And this is not, I think, a mere counsel of necessity. For when one has the Church, then one also has the faith of the Church, and so one has everything.

Chesterton's Anglican Churchmanship

Chesterton was, of course, concerned with the Church long before he entered peace and communion with the See of Rome. In his Anglo-Catholic period his churchmanship was, however, not terribly engaged, except in controversy. Surprisingly, he seems to have participated very little in the rich liturgical life of the Anglo-Catholic parishes to which his wife's faithfulness of practice and his own reputation as an Anglo-Catholic Sir Galahad would surely have given him ready access. This should not prevent us from taking seriously the ecclesiological elements in his earlier works, and above all in *Orthodoxy*'s sixth chapter, 'The Paradoxes of Christianity' which, while it hardly touches on the structure of the Church – as organic community, hierarchical society, or whatever, has plenty to say about the Church's life – moral, ascetical, devotional, credal.

Ecclesial paradox in *Orthodoxy*

In *Orthodoxy* Chesterton recounts how struck he was by the contrariety of the objections brought against the Church for being both deplorably X and lamentably non-X at one and the same time. This is where the application to ecclesiology of the famous Chestertonian love of paradox comes into its own.[5] If, pondered Chesterton, recreating the mind-set of his uncommitted days:

> [T]his mass of mad contradictions really existed, quakerish and blood-thirsty, too gorgeous and too thread-bare, austere, yet pandering preposterously to the lust of the eye, the enemy of women and their foolish refuge, a solemn pessimist and a silly optimist, if this evil existed, then there was in this evil something quite supreme and unique ... Such a paradox of evil rose to the stature of the supernatural ... An historic institution, which never went right, is really quite as much of a miracle as an institution that cannot go wrong.[6]

Chesterton's first reaction was, 'Perhaps Christ – and therefore the Church of Christ – is the Antichrist.' His second reaction was, if a man is criticised for being the wrong shape by critics who flatly contradict each other in their attempts to say just what is wrong about him, quite possibly he is quite the right shape after all. In Chesterton's example:

> [I]t was certainly odd that the modern world charged Christianity at once with bodily austerity and with artistic pomp. But then it was also odd, very odd, that the modern world itself combined extreme bodily luxury with an extreme absence of artistic pomp. The modern man thought Becket's robes too rich and his meals too poor. But then the modern man was really exceptional in history; no man before ever ate such elaborate dinners in such ugly clothes.[7]

Thinking constructively on the point, Chesterton divined that the Church had maintained the Aristotelian insight that virtue lies in a 'mean', a middle way, in Greek *meson*. But she had understood this in an altogether distinctive fashion. She had understood it to mean a 'moderation made from

5. Y. Denis, *G. K. Chesterton. Paradoxe et Catholicisme*, Paris, Les Belles Lettres, 1978.
6. G. K. Chesterton, *Orthodoxy*, London, Hodder & Stoughton, 1996, p. 129. The original edition is from 1908.
7. Ibid., pp. 130–1.

the still crash of two impetuous emotions'.[8] The key lies, he thought, in the overall Gospel message about creation, fall, and redemption, which furnishes us with two contrasting yet not for that reason mutually exclusive truths. Chesterton writes:

> In one way Man was to be haughtier than he had ever been before; in another way he was to be humbler than he had ever been before. In so far as I am Man I am the chief of creatures. In so far as I am a man I am the chief of sinners. Christianity thus held a thought of the dignity of man that could only be expressed in crowns rayed like the sun and fans of peacock plumage. Yet at the same time it could hold a thought about the abject smallness of man that could only be expressed in fasting and fantastic submission, in the gray ashes of St Dominic and the white snows of St Bernard.[9]

Francis of Assisi in his praise of good could be a more blatant optimist than Whitman; Jerome of Bethlehem, in his denunciation of evil, could be a blacker pessimist than Schopenhauer. And the explanation is that 'both passions were free because both were kept in their place'.[10]

The 'historic Church' has emphasised both celibacy and the family. It has told some men to fight and others not to fight. It has sanctioned both asceticism and celebration – and each in relation to the other.

> Because a man prayed and fasted on the Northern snows, flowers could be flung at his festival in the Southern cities; and because fanatics drank water on the sands of Syria, men could still drink cider in the orchards of England.[11]

Care in the formulation of doctrine

'Mental and emotional liberty', observed Chesterton, 'are not so simple as they look.'[12] The Church 'had to be careful',

8. Ibid., p. 135.
9. Ibid., pp. 136–7.
10. Ibid., p. 139.
11. Ibid., p. 144.
12. Ibid., p. 138.

not least so that the 'world might be careless'.[13] Hence
the great care that had to be invested in the formulation
of doctrine. The Church 'went in specifically for dangerous
ideas; she was a lion-tamer'.[14]

> The idea of birth through a Holy Spirit, of the death of a divine
> being, of the forgiveness of sins, or the fulfilment of prophe-
> cies, are ideas which, any one can see, need but a touch to turn
> them into something blasphemous or ferocious. The smallest
> link was let drop by the artificers of the Mediterranean [Ches-
> terton is referring to the bishop-theologians, chiefly Greek- and
> Latin-speaking, who formulated the Creeds and other doctrinal
> formulae], and the lion of ancestral pessimism burst his chain
> in the forgotten forests of the North [i. e. among the newly con-
> verted Germanic peoples].[15]

The Church taught Chesterton that the 'thrilling romance
of Orthodoxy' is also a remarkable sanity. But, as he adds,
'to be sane is more dramatic than to be mad': it is the 'equi-
librium of a man behind madly rushing horses'.[16] It was in
that spirit that he 'accepted Christendom' as his 'mother'.[17]
A 'living teacher', it (or she):

> not only certainly taught me yesterday, but will almost certainly
> teach me tomorrow.[18]

Evidently, he expected further truths from the treasury of
the deposit of faith to strike home before he died.

The atmosphere of a fresh conversion

What Chesterton did not know in 1908, though the play he
makes between the words 'romance' and 'Rome' perhaps
indicates some surmise, was that Christendom would teach
him the wider circle of truths into which he entered in 1922

[13.] Ibid., p. 146.
[14.] Ibid., p. 145.
[15.] Ibid.
[16.] Ibid., p. 146.
[17.] Ibid., p. 232.
[18.] Ibid., p. 230.

with his move from the Church of England to the Catholic Church.

One cannot imagine Chesterton at any time of his life as glued to church newspapers or perusing pastoral letters. Like Evelyn Waugh, he probably regarded a detailed interest in ecclesiastical affairs on the part of laymen as a telltale sign of incipient lunacy. As he put it, more gently, in *The Catholic Church and Conversion*:

> [I]n most communions the ecclesiastical layman is more ecclesiastical than is good for his health, and certainly much more ecclesiastical than the ecclesiastics.[19]

Even so, it is not surprising that his conversion to Catholicism triggered a new phase of writing of a more focused ecclesiological kind. This was a momentous shift of allegiance to a form of Christianity which, in England, had been, ever since the seventeenth century, deeply unpopular or at any rate suspect. After the failure of the second Jacobite uprising in 1745, the spread of Enlightenment tolerance combined with the discretion of the recusant minority to improve matters. But the situation was soon re-inflamed with the nineteenth-century mass immigration of Irish paupers and the fears of crypto-Romanism in the Church of England the Tractarian and Ritualist movements enkindled. Dislike of Catholicism has been called, no doubt too cynically, the default religion of the English. Its last dramatic public manifestation (so far) was in the year when Chesterton published *Orthodoxy*, 1908. An international Eucharistic Congress was held in London. The Metropolitan Police announced they would be unable to guarantee public order if the monstrance containing the Eucharistic host were carried through the streets of the capital.

Would such ill-will have worried Chesterton? *Did* it worry him? Did he, as some think, fear a diminution of Englishness? Well, the problem was scarcely confined to England. He noted later 'the sincere and savage hatred felt by many

---

[19]. G. K. Chesterton, *The Catholic Church and Conversion*, London, Burns, Oates and Washbourne, 1926, p. 40.

Europeans for the religion of their own European past'.[20]
And in any case, like John Henry Newman when writing the
Essay on the Development of Christian Doctrine, he was
inclined to think that the penchant of the Catholic Church
for attracting hostility was a sign of its identity with the
Church of early Christian times. The story of the Church is,
he thought:

> the story of ... something which is always coming out of the
> Catacombs and going back again, something that is never
> entirely acceptable when it appears, and never entirely forgot-
> ten when it disappears.[21]

His apologia

Chesterton's principal apologia was, as its title suggests, his
1926 *The Catholic Church and Conversion*. But two essay
collections throw further light on his thinking: *The Thing*, of
1929, and *The Well and the Shallows*, from 1935, the year
before his death.

Among other things, *The Catholic Church and Conversion* sought to deconstruct the English, British, or
Anglo-Saxon tradition of popular anti-Catholicism: a necessary step if Chesterton were to capture the good will of
his readership.[22] Newman, who had much the same aims as
Chesterton in his *Lectures on the Present Position of Catholics in England*, parodies anti-Catholicism with almost
Dickensian *grotesquerie*,[23] whereas Chesterton, who by
his own confession, had never felt the full force of the anti-
Catholic tradition, shows a lighter touch.[24] Of more significance for the faith of the universal Church is the way

---

[20.] G. K. Chesterton, *The Glass Walking-stick, and Other Essays*, London,
Methuen, 1955, p. 60.

[21.] Ibid., p. 63.

[22.] See P. Jenkins, 'Chesterton and the Anti-Catholic Tradition', *The Chesterton Review* XVIII. 3, 1992, pp. 345–70.

[23.] I. Ker, *The Catholic Revival in English Literature (1845–1961). Newman, Hopkins, Belloc, Chesterton, Greene, Waugh*, Notre Dame, Ind.,
University of Notre Dame Press, 2003, p. 22.

[24.] G. K. Chesterton, *The Catholic Church and Conversion*, p. 16.

Chesterton treats the arguments, as distinct from preju-
dices, which inhibit access to Catholicism. He shows how,
in a number of cases, these arguments, by their diametri-
cal opposition one to another, have a marked tendency to
cancel each other out. Thus, for example, the universalist
curses Rome for 'having too much predestination', the Cal-
vinist curses her for 'having too little', one 'No Popery man'
finds her doctrine of Purgatory 'too tender-hearted', another
finds her doctrine of Hell 'too harsh'.[25] This state of affairs
is exactly analogous to the situation Chesterton found to
be the case with objections to 'Christendom' in *Orthodoxy*,
where he concluded that someone found so inconsistently
to be always wrong might actually be right.

What holds more people back is, he thinks, not so much
metaphysics as morals. The sense of moral demand found in
a Church that uses auricular confession in its administration
of Penance, and, more widely, wields pastoral authority in
the service of a clear moral code, is something challenging
– and, therefore, daunting to the unexamined or comfort-
ably mediocre life. The expectation of realistic sincerity in
the confessional frightens people, for the very good reason
that 'most modern realists only like [realism] because they
are careful to be realistic about *other* people'.[26] And, more
widely, the convert will have to be more responsible:

> He will have somebody to be responsible to and he will know
> what he is responsible for; two uncomfortable conditions
> which his more fortunate fellow creatures have nowadays
> entirely escaped.[27]

Once these obstacles are overcome – if they *are* overcome
– the person is free to discover the Church, a process Chesterton describes as easier than joining it and much easier
than trying to live its life. He compares the discovery to
finding 'a new continent full of strange flowers and fantas-

[25.] Ibid., p. 36.
[26.] Ibid., p. 38.
[27.] Ibid., p. 39.

tic animals, which is at once wild and hospitable'.[28] There
now intervenes, so Chesterton claims in what we can call
his phenomenology of the conversion process, an 'interval
of intense nervousness' before someone takes the plunge,
rather as with the shaky bridegroom at the wedding or the
army recruit who takes the king's shilling and gets drunk
partly to celebrate but partly to forget. Its content is anxiety
that what previously seemed so bad as to be intolerable
now seems too good to be true. But if nonetheless someone
actually joins the Catholic Church, Chesterton predicts the
chief effect will be one of stepping into a larger room.

> At the last moment of all, the convert often feels as if he were
> looking through a leper's window. He is looking through a little
> crack or crooked hole that seems to grow smaller as he stares
> at it; but it is an opening that looks towards the Altar. Only,
> when he has entered the Church, he finds that the Church is
> much larger inside than it is outside. He has left behind him the
> lop-sidedness of lepers' windows and even in a sense the nar-
> rowness of Gothic doors; and he is under vast domes as open as
> the Renaissance and as universal as the Republic of the world.[29]

Entering a wider realm

The experience of entering this wider space is discussed
by Chesterton under the heading 'The world inside out'.
The basic idea here is that revelation as transmitted in the
Catholic Church is the greatest possible truth that can be
conceived. (There is, incidentally, an affinity with the theological apologetics of the great twentieth-century Swiss
dogmatician Hans Urs von Balthasar in this remark.) All
other truths, whatever their provenance, can fit into this
truth but it cannot fit into them. In *The Thing* Chesterton
applies this to Calvinists who 'took the Catholic idea of the
absolute knowledge and power of God', and to Evangelicals
who 'seized on the very Catholic idea that mankind has a
sense of sin',[30] but also to those outside Christianity in any

[28.] Ibid., p. 45.
[29.] Ibid., p. 49.
[30.] G. K. Chesterton, *The Thing*, p. 29.

form – such as the atheistic poets Shelley and Whitman and
the 'revolutionary optimists' (presumably, from the Great
Revolution of the West, 1789–1815) – who had:

> taken out of the old Catholic tradition one particular transcen-
> dental idea; the idea that there is a spiritual dignity in man as
> man, and a universal duty to love men as men.[31]

That was the nugget of gold which Chesterton, following
Belloc's example, extracted from the French revolutionar-
ies' 'Declaration of the Rights of Man and of the Citizen'.
Many elements of Catholic truth, then, are found outside
Catholicism altogether. As Chesterton puts it in *The Catholic
Church and Conversion*:

> [The convert] is not worried by being told that there is
> something in Spiritualism or something in Christian Science.
> He knows there is something in everything. But he is moved
> by the more impressive fact that he finds everything in
> something.[32]

If that is somewhat oracular, Chesterton spells it out when
he writes:

> The outsiders stand by and see, or think they see, the convert
> entering with bowed head a sort of small temple which they
> are convinced is fitted up inside like a prison, if not a torture-
> chamber.But all they really know about it is that he has passed
> through a door. They do not know that he has not gone into
> the inner darkness, but out into the broad daylight. It is he who
> is, in the broad and beautiful sense of the word, an outsider.
> He does not want to go into a larger room, because he does
> not know of any larger room to go into. He knows of a large
> number of much smaller rooms, each of which is labelled as
> being very large; but he is quite sure he would be cramped in
> any of them. Each of them professes to be a complete cosmos or
> scheme of all things ... Each of them is supposed to be domed
> with the sky or painted inside with all the stars. But each of
> these cosmic systems or machines seems to him much smaller

---

31. Ibid., p. 30.
32. G. K. Chesterton, *The Catholic Church and Conversion*, p. 67.

and even much simpler than the broad and balanced universe in which he lives.[33]

That is, clearly, the Chesterton of *Orthodoxy* speaking and it justifies, up to a point, the claim of the Canadian Chesterton scholar Ian Boyd that Chesterton's conversion 'was the result of a personal decision that had more to do with a question of fact than a change in his religious convictions'.[34] But what fact? Chesterton tells us himself in *The Catholic Church and Conversion* when he writes:

> There are High Churchmen as much as Low Churchmen who are concerned first and last to save the Church of England. Some of them think it can be saved by calling it Catholic, or making it Catholic, or believing that it is Catholic; but *that* is what they want to save. But I did not start out with the idea of saving the English Church, but of finding the Catholic Church. If the two were one, so much the better; but I had never conceived of Catholicism as a sort of showy attribute or attraction to be tacked on to my own national body, but as the inmost soul of the true body, wherever it might be. It might be said [concluded Chesterton] that Anglo-Catholicism was simply my own uncompleted conversion to Catholicism.[35]

In the early twenty-first century when classical Anglo-Catholics are profoundly shaken by defections from historic Christian faith and order in the Anglican Communion, Chesterton's perspective has lost nothing of its pertinence to a future re-configuration of Anglophone Catholicity in the West. 'Does the reader know', asked the Chesterton student David Fagerberg:

> the optical illusion in which if one looks at black on white one sees a vase, but if one blinks and looks at white on black one sees two faces? Chesterton was sketching a vase to hold the flowers of his philosophy, and when he blinked, he

[33.] Ibid., p. 68.
[34.] I. Boyd, *The Novels of G. K. Chesterton. A Study in Art and Propoaganda*, London, Elek, 1975, p. xii.
[35.] G. K. Chesterton, *The Catholic Church and Conversion*, p. 19.

saw the face of a human, ecclesial community (and it had a Roman nose).[36]

A last look back

That was in 1926, though. How did things appear ten years later, at the end of his life? The best guide is *The Well and the Shallows* published the year before he died where Chesterton looks back on the intervening decade to discuss what he calls his 'post-conversion conversion'. In these pages he registers further developments in culture and society that, he believes:

> would in any case have rendered impossible any intellectual position outside the [Roman Catholic] Church, and especially the position in which I originally found myself.[37]

Commenting on the rise of the European dictators and the revival of militant anti-clericalism in Spain, Chesterton found democratic modernity to be exhausting the moral capital the West has inherited from the ages of faith. This was an anticipation on his part of the recent, if tardy, interest in cultural analysis on the part of the Catholic magisterium. It was also in keeping with his earlier claims that humanism may be the pool, but Christendom is the fountain.

> [I]n the centre of the civilisation called Catholic, there and in no movement and in no future, is found that crystallisation of commonsense and true traditions and rational reforms, for which the modern man mistakenly looked to the trend of the modern age.[38]

Furthermore, Chesterton noted the steadily progressing heterogeneous deformation of the main Protestant bodies.

[36.] D. W. Fagerberg, *The Size of Chesterton's Catholicism*, Notre Dame, Ind, and London, University of Notre Dame Press 1998, p. 184.

[37.] G. K. Chesterton, *The Well and the Shallows*, London, Sheed and Ward, 1935, p. 23.

[38.] Ibid., p. 35.

A process he called the 'fossilisation' of Protestantism was evidenced by the growth of Anglican Modernism on the one hand and, on the other, the rise of the Nazi-sponsored so-called 'German Christianity' across the North Sea. 'Fossilisation' seems an odd term for vigorous if misguided religious movements, but Chesterton explains its use here well enough when he writes:

> A fossil is not a dead animal, or a decayed organism, or in essence even an antiquated object. The whole point of a fossil is that it is the *form* of an animal or organism, from which all its own animal or organic substance has entirely disappeared; but which has kept its shape, because it has been filled up by some totally different substance by some process of distillation or secretion, so that we might almost say, as in the mediaeval metaphysics, that its substance has vanished and only its accidents remain.[39]

The substance of Christianity is evaporating, Chesterton was claiming, from the historic churches of the Reformation. So far as the Church of England was concerned, the 1930 Lambeth Conference's opening the way to contraceptive practice and a series of straws in the wind indicating a future acceptance of divorce deepened the sense of disillusion already growing since the Prayer Book crisis of 1928. The re-assertion by the British Parliament of its right to determine the public worship of the Church – and the Church's acquiescence therein – struck Chesterton as an alien claim to 'ownership' of an Anglican Christian's mind.[40] A State Church, if the legislature of the State in question was itself non-Anglican, must be, he now thought, a monstrosity and the wider Anglican Communion too affected by the forces of a flawed public opinion to count as a satisfactory counterweight.

We could sum up the temper of Chesterton's Catholicism in his last year with the words that give *The Well and the Shallows* its title:

> We have come out of the shallows and the dry places to the one deep well; and the Truth is at the bottom of it.[41]

[39] Ibid., p. 25.
[40] Ibid., p. 45.
[41] Ibid., p. 72.

Looking back, doubtless on his own career as well as that of others', Chesterton noted:

> We have done far less than we should have done, to explain all that balance of subtlety and sanity which is meant by a Christian civilization ... We did not ourselves think that the mere denial of our dogmas could end in such dehumanised and demented anarchy ... We did not believe that rationalists were so utterly mad until they made it quite clear to us ... We have done very little against them; *non nobis, Domine*; the glory of their final overthrow is all their own.[42]

Conclusion

As Chesterton's treatment of this subject indicates, if Chesterton is to be a *doctor Ecclesiae* (and this, if it happens, will be for more areas of revelation-relevant understanding than are covered here – my *G. K. Chesterton, Theologian* attempts further exploration), he will chiefly be a controversialist doctor, like, say, Cyril of Alexandria or Robert Bellarmine, which is not to say that his theological gifts are merely acute, rather than deep. I believe Chesterton enjoyed contemplative gifts of a high order, and notably the Gift of the Holy Spirit that Scripture calls 'Wisdom'. Otherwise, the unerring rectitude of the judgements in so many areas of one was who hardly even an auto-didact in the study of divinity is scarcely explicable. Still, he will remain, true to his charism, a knight who jousts with dragons. His theological doctrine is not stated simply for its own sake but so as to make an impact in the realm of culture, which is to say, to shake out of their present sensibilities those who minds and hearts are closed to revelation – or at any rate to revelation as carried by the Catholic Church – through the effect of 'what the media say'. But just such a doctor is the kind who, as the twenty-first century gets into its stride in England (and not only here), we most need to identify and make our own.

What commends him above all is the spaciousness of his Christian mind, the range of his experiential materials, the sense he conveys of Catholicism as a wider room

42. Ibid., p. 79.

than any of the competing 'isms' of religious – or, for that matter, secular – history. No one has written better of the gift of creation, the mystical quality of 'ordinary' life, the fulfilling of the pagan in the Christian, the practicality of a religion that synthesizes doctrine, ritual, and the everyday, the way the puzzle of the world and of life requires a revelation at once complex and single-minded to solve it, the liberating function of dogma for the imagination, and the self-defeating quality of schism. In a difficult age of the Church such as our own, when the invidious choice is often between, on the one hand, the vague and woolly whose religion is hardly more than humanism with a spiritual tinge, and, on the other, cribbed and cramped *zelanti*, he is surely the apologist-doctor of the hour. We can afford to wait a while for his elevation, for the 'hour' in question will be long.

Was Chesterton a Mystic? – I

Nicholas Madden

If we are to discover whether or not Chesterton can appropriately be described as a 'mystic', we must first establish
the meaning of the word and the related ways in which it
is used. It is generally acknowledged that 'mysticism' is not
an unambiguous term. Here it will be used in a Christian
sense. Although there is no agreement on what the term
means, there is a consensus among scholars that with the
Spanish Carmelites of the sixteenth century, Teresa of Avila
and John of the Cross, we find what is acknowledged to
be an exemplary expression of mysticism understood as a
nuanced experience of the supernatural.

St Teresa is sometimes charged with having introduced
too much psychological description in her accounts of how
she apprehended the presence of the divine in her life.
Misericordias Domini in aeternum cantabo (The mercies
of the Lord I will sing for ever) was how this Doctor of the
Church understood what she was doing, and who better to
define it? It has been said of her *Interior Castle* that it is 'a
lesson in spiritual theology, which changes itself smoothly
into a treatise on mystical theology, written by a woman
who had experienced and thought deeply about her own
spiritual and mystical process. From that she is capable of
lifting herself from the narrative to the doctrinal plane and
of codifying in her own way the journey of the Christian to
the plenitude of Christological and Trinitarian life, in the
function of the Church'.[1]

A glance at the contents of this masterpiece will give us

---

[1] Tomas Alvarez in *Diccionario de Santa Teresa, Doctrina e Historia*,
Burgos, 2002, p. 137. My translation.

a hint of what it contains and why it exemplifies mystical writing in classical form. Teresa's language is more spontaneous than technical. She was familiar with traditional ways of expressing herself, but she was also markedly original and reminds us that it is one thing to have supernatural experience but another to have the grace to express it. The door of entry to the castle is prayer and then follows the sequence of mansions. There is no entering by proxy. The person must engage with God in a personal way in prayer. This will be accompanied by self-knowledge. The next phase is marked by 'struggle' with the disordered tendencies that persist. However there is a progressive sensibility in listening to the Word of God. The proving of love is shown in overcoming egoism, a new pattern of spiritual living and the beginnings of apostolic zeal. This is paradoxically enhanced by aridity. The Fourth Mansions are distinguished by a transition to mystical experience, even if intermittent. We find the mind enlightened and the will quiet in passive love. This transition is followed by a state of union and sustained conformity of the will to God. Teresa uses the image of the silkworm that dies and emerges transformed to illustrate the person's rebirth in Christ. This is expressed especially in love of the neighbour. The following stage has been described as a crucible of love where the tension of theological life can take on a purgatorial character. There is a keen awareness of the presence of the Word made flesh. Here Teresa uses marital symbolism to describe the relationship of the soul to God. It is the time of engagement. This culminates in 'mystical marriage'. It means total insertion in the Christological and Trinitarian mysteries, accompanied by 'a hunger for the honour of God', 'a hunger to lead souls to Him like St Dominic and St Francis , like the Crucified one.'[2]

One quotation will convey the quality of what takes place 'in the extreme interior, is some place very deep within', as Teresa perceived it:

When the soul is brought into that dwelling place, the Most Blessed Trinity, all three Persons, through an intellectual

[2] Ibid., p. 138.

vision, is revealed to it through a certain representation of the
truth … It knows in such a way that what we hold by faith, it
understands, we can say, through sight – although the sight is
not with the bodily eyes nor with the eyes of the soul, because
we are not dealing with an imaginative vision. Here all three
Persons communicate themselves to it, speak to it, explain
those words of the Lord in the Gospel: that He and the Father
and the Holy Spirit will come to dwell with the soul that loves
Him and keeps His commandments.[3]

St Teresa was no stranger to mystical phenomena like
ecstasy, rapture, visions and locutions, but what she wanted
for her nuns above all was stabilised charity, 'the greatest of
these' (1 Cor 13). It is also important to keep in mind the
theological focus of her experience.

In a magisterial article on mysticism in the *Dictionnaire
de Spiritualité* we find three criteria of mystical experience: *pati divina* (experiencing or undergoing the divine),
la purification passive (passive purification) and *l'union
théopathique*.[4] The first is a Latin version of Dionysius'
formula by which he designates a knowledge that comes
from experience as opposed to what comes by study and
is considered to be an essential qualification in the mystic's
curriculum vitae. The initiate, under the influence of divine
inspiration, not only grasps, 'but undergoes divine things'.[5]
It is pointed out that St John of the Cross considers that the
mystical life, properly speaking, begins with the onset of the
night of spirit. This varies from case to case, so to speak. *Periti*
consider that St Thérèse of Lisieux entered it unexpectedly
about a year and a half before she died and it remained until
she was at the point of death. (This raises questions which
cannot be pursued here – did she not, for instance, enjoy
union before this and if so what was the significance of this

3. Teresa of Avila, *The Interior Castle*, vol. 2,1,6 in *The Collected Works of
St Teresa of Avila*, vol. 2, tr. Kieran Kavanaugh OCD and Otilio Rodriguez OCD, Washington, ICS Publications, 1980, p. 428.
4. *Dictionnaire de Spiritualité*, vol. 10, Paul Agasse and Michael Sales,
Paris, Beauchesne, 1955–1984.
5. *The Divine Names* in Pseudo-Dionysius, *The Complete Works*, tr. Colm
Luibheid, New York, Paulist Press, 1987, p. 65.

trial?) The development of the mystical life typically issues in union with God. Contemplatives who have experience of this agree on two points: It is impossible to enjoy this privilege without having undergone a thorough purification of sense and spirit, a return to 'the state of innocence';[6] the preparation does not necessarily culminate in union – this is something totally gratuitous on the part of God and recognised by the recipient to be so. We can say provisionally that we have no evidence that Chesterton thought that he had been through this kind of experience. He would probably have laughed heartily at the suggestion.

Here it is fitting to recall that there are at least two schools of thought as to what constitutes Christian mysticism, with big names on both sides. On the one side we have those who consider mysticism to be something 'extraordinary', while on the other we have the champions of what Rahner called 'everyday mysticism'. Rahner takes notice of the kind of experience described by John of the Cross, which he admits to being a 'special', knowledge , 'for it consists of a certain touch of the Divinity and so it is God himself who is felt and tasted there, although not clearly and in a manifest way, as in glory'.[7] But, in a brilliant passage, he describes 'experiencing the Spirit in Actual Life' in a series of credible situations which are glaringly ordinary and claims that:

> There is God and his liberating grace ... There is the mysticism of everyday life, the discovery of God in all things; there is sober intoxication of the Spirit, of which the Fathers and liturgy speak which we cannot reject or despise, because it is real.[8]

It is to be noted that he claims the authority of the Fathers and of the liturgy for his interpretation of 'mysticism'

---

6. San Juan de la Cruz, *Obras Completas*, Madrid, Editorial de Espiritualidad, 1980, p. 1161 in which he refers to 'the state of original justice in which God gave to Adam grace and innocence'. My translation.
7. St John of the Cross, *The Ascent of Mount Carmel* in *The Collected Works of St John of the Cross*, tr. Kieran Kavanaugh OCD and Otilio Rodriguez OCD, Washington, ICS Publications, 1973, p. 195.
8. Karl Rahner, *The Practice of Faith*, eds Karl Lehmann and Albert Raffelt, New York, SCM Press Ltd, 1982, p. 70.

without adducing proof from the Fathers and the liturgy. Has Rahner forgotten Gregory of Nyssa, for instance or his own noteworthy essay on Origen's 'spiritual senses'? An expression like 'everyday mysticism' would seem to fudge the issue as if one were to claim that prose is 'everyday poetry'. The final trial of St Thérèse of Lisieux has been adduced as an instance of 'everyday mysticism'. Federico Ruiz thinks that

> St Thérèse of Lisieux lived the dark night in a contemplative Carmelite context, very like that of St John of the Cross. She presents similar signs of the darkness of faith, temptations to blasphemy, thinking existence to be a nonsense. But she puts forward a variation, which not even as a hypothesis happens to the protagonist of St John's description. The darkness of faith is translated, in the ambient of the sanjuanistic work, as fear that God has abandoned or not pardoned him; the subject has doubts about himself, not about God. Thérèse lives her darkness of faith with another more radical symptom: the fear, the suspicion, the thought that God does not exist, nor is there a heaven, and all is a dream. Between St John and St Thérèse there are three centuries of atheism. And the cultural ambient puts pressure on individuals.[9]

There is an intensity in the suffering of the saint and a simultaneous joy that baffles the everyday mystic. Towards the end she said: 'No, I could never have believed it possible to have suffered so much! Never! Never! I can explain it only by the ardent desires I had to save souls.'[10] When she was eleven years of age she said

> I felt myself flooded with consolations so great that I look upon them as on of the greatest graces of my life. Suffering became my attraction; it had charms about it which ravished me without my understanding them very well.[11]

From then on she would learn and with the unusual nuance

9. San Juan de la Cruz, *Obras Completas*, p. 512. My translation.

10. St Thérèse of Lisieux, *Her Last Conversations*, tr. John Clarke OCD, Washington DC, ICS Publications, 1977, p. 15.

11. St Thérèse of Lisieux, *The Story of a Soul*, tr. John Clarke OCD, Washington DC, ICS Publications, 1996, p. 79.

of loving that from which we recoil. Apart from other evidence in her writings and the testimony of witnesses for her canonisation, this alone ironically would seem to put the saint of 'the little way' in the 'extraordinary' category of mystics. Ironically, it is known that Chesterton did not seem to have had much affinity with St Thérèse.

Without presuming to adjudicate between the exponents of two interpretations of 'mysticism', for the purposes of this essay we shall try to see G. K. Chesterton's claim to be a mystic in the strict sense as outlined above. He would probably have little trouble in qualifying for the title, if judged in the light of the alternative exegesis, as proposed for instance by Rahner. Maisie Ward, as appears from the following, was keen to dub Chesterton a 'mystic':

> The Everlasting Man and St. Francis seem to me the highest expression of Gilbert's mysticism. I have hesitated to use the word for it is not one to be used lightly, but I can find no other. Like most Catholics I have been wont to believe that to be a mystic a man must first be an ascetic and Gilbert was not an ascetic in the ordinary sense. But is there not for the thinker an asceticism of the mind, very searching, very purifying? In his youth he had told Bentley that creative writing was the hardest of hard labour; that sense of the pressure of thought that made Newman call creative writing 'getting rid of pain by pain'; the profound depression that follows; the exhaustion that seems like a bottomless pit. St Theresa said that the hardest penance was easier than mental prayer: was not much of Gilbert's thought a contemplation.[12]

However, in *Return to Chesterton*, p. 42, she tells us that 'it was always easier for Gilbert to make a strenuous mental effort than a physical one'. It would be hard to find a better argument in favour of allowing him the title, but perhaps Ms Ward's original estimate of the term 'ascetic' was sounder than her plea for the thinker's experience as meeting that requirement. We know from Frank Harris that wine and companionship had the effect of endowing him with astonishing

---

[12.] Maisie Ward, *Gilbert Keith Chesterton*, London, Sheed & Ward, 1944, pp. 410–11.

verbal inspiration. Besides, she seems gratuitously to equate Chesterton's contemplation with mental prayer.

There is no gainsaying Chesterton's genius, bristling with originality, his wholesome goodness, his generous humour, his massive modesty. In the chapter entitled 'How to be a Lunatic' in his autobiography, we find an almost defiant profession of faith in the Roman Catholic Church, with its creeds and dogmas and sacraments. For instance, 'I am very proud of being orthodox about the mysteries of the Trinity or the Mass; I am proud of believing in the Confessional; I am proud of believing in the Papacy.'[13] For him to read the Gospels was to feel as if rocks were rolled on him,[14] he venerated Mary, revelling in Theotokos,[15] pride was not one of his sins, he thought 'but laziness, yes, and certain kinds of anger';[16] after his First Communion he admitted that 'I have spent the happiest hour of my life';[17] he was imbued with a profound reverence and awe with regard to confession and holy communion – communion made him happy – 'and yet next time it's just the same again: the same dread, the same difficulty and reluctance'.[18] These brief indications reveal a good man endowed with a strong faith, accompanied by an unusual appreciation of what it gave him. Then, remarkable appreciation seems to have been a characteristic of his thinking from those absorptions of his youth up to his writing of St Thomas Aquinas. Referring to the Modernists he wrote:

> Now what we have really got to hammer into the heads of all these people, somehow, is that a thinking man can think himself deeper and deeper into Catholicism, and not deeper and deeper into difficulties about Catholicism.[19]

[13.] G. K. Chesterton, *The Autobiography of G. K. Chesterton*, San Francisco, Ignatius Press, 2000, p. 87.

[14.] Maisie Ward, *Gilbert Keith Chesterton*, p. 407.

[15.] G. K. Chesterton, *The Thing*, London, Sheed & Ward, 1931, p. 217.

[16.] Maisie Ward, *Return to Chesterton*, London, Sheed and Ward, 1952, p. 244.

[17.] Maisie Ward, *Gilbert Keith Chesterton*, p. 530.

[18.] Maisie Ward, *Return to Chesterton*, p. 245.

[19.] G. K. Chesterton, *The Thing*, p. 212.

The grasp, the insight, the originality, the delight, mark everything he expressed, his detective stories, his controversial writing, his biographies, his conversation with children, his brilliance as a debater, his poetry, his faith in search of understanding. We might try to sum it up by saying that his thought was a stream of realisations, striking, paradoxical, profound. Referring to *Orthodoxy*, Wilfrid Ward said that 'To see [the great thoughts of Christianity] strike with all the force of youth on a gifted mind makes them young again to us.'[20] And this gift was evident, no matter what the object of his thought, whether in the realm of nature or of grace. It seems that he did not read many books; 'for genius, hints and winks are enough'; he could 'reach into the interiorities of something he had just heard of'.[21] Chesterton was undoubtedly a man of capacious spirit, but realisations are not encounters and encounters with the divine seem to be at the core of Christian mysticism in its strictest sense. There is no denying his wisdom. He evidently has that *sapor* which delights in genuine knowledge, whatever its provenance. *Proxime accessit*: he comes close; but does he have the distinctive gift that would win him the epithet which would seem to be required here? A glance at the *Shorter Oxford English Dictionary* will assure us that 'mystic' and cognate terms are by no means unambiguous. In a haphazard scale from initiate into mysteries down to obscurity and delusion, we find allegorical, occult, esoteric, enigmatic, awe-inspiring, having spiritual import, non-rational access to knowledge and more. We seem to be getting nearer to familiar ground with 'one who seeks by contemplation and self surrender to obtain union with or absorption into the Deity'. Generally speaking, it was not Chesterton's way to define his terms and so we find him using the notion of mysticism differently in different contexts, tapping into the variety just mentioned. As a young man he visualised a mystical entity which he calls 'the wonder, the holy, the highest',[22] which seems to require a vague condition in which one

---

[20.] Quoted in William Oddie, *Chesterton and the Romance of Orthodoxy*, Oxford, Oxford University Press, 2008, p. 360.

[21.] Rann Kennedy quoted in Maisie Ward, *Return to Chesterton*, p. 69.

[22.] Oddie, *Chesterton and the Romance of Orthodoxy*, p. 96.

might pluck the silver apples of the moon, the golden apples of the sun. This idealism embraced the enjoyment of the 'brotherhood of men',[23] later perceived as 'a mystical dogma'. In describing his escape from the vortex of subjectivism and nihilism, he hints that he has talked to God face to face and found 'a mystically satisfactory state of things', which seems to be the beginnings of the critical realism[24] that would be confirmed by Aquinas whose 'special spiritual thesis' was that 'there really are Things, and not only the Thing'.[25] He sought the universal through the particular, an exercise based on the sacramental principle. This source of wonder was to become a basic in all his thinking: 'There is one secret in life/The secret of constant astonishment'.[26] He would say later on: 'The object of the artistic and spiritual life was to dig for this submerged sunrise of wonder.' For Belloc,

> He excelled in what is not an English characteristic, but one which he could introduce to his fellow-citizens with an ease that one more alien could never have enjoyed; I mean the element of precision and of deductive reasoning. It was this, that rational process of the mind, which governed all his development in the matter of religion.[27]

Wonder and the sensorium of the transcendent were served by logic rather than by the emotional or the experiential. Alfred Noyes remarked that 'It is the element of strangeness in familiar things rather than that of beauty, that is most potent to bring Mr. Chesterton into the heart of the world's mystery.'[28] Elsewhere he thinks that it is his mission 'to interpret to us the infinite love and mercy of that secret but very present God'.[29] The basic temper of Chesterton's

23. Ibid.
24. Ibid., p. 124.
25. G. K. Chesterton, *St. Thomas Aquinas*, London, Hodder & Stoughton Ltd., 1933, p. 159.
26. Oddie, *Chesterton and the Romance of Orthodoxy*, p. 152.
27. Ibid., p. 185.
28. Ibid., p. 229.
29. Ibid., p. 234.

mind was gratitude. In his *Autobiography* he tells us that 'he had hung on to religion by one thin thread of thanks'.[30] He uses the term 'mystical' in a more comprehensive religious sense when he refers to the Incarnation and 'a large number of other mystical dogmas ranging from the mystical dogma that man is the image of God to the mystical dogma that all men are equal, and that babies should not be strangled'.[31] Having referred to the 'superhuman', the 'spiritualistic' and 'doctrine' in speaking about the Nicene Creed and more specifically about Christmas he writes: 'It seems strange that a dogma of mystics should be the only thing which will make grown-up people play Blind Man's buff'.[32] Even more outrageously the dominical paradox that it is the one who loses his life who will save it 'is not a piece of mysticism for saints and heroes. It is a piece of everyday advice for sailors and mountaineers'.[33] 'Mystics' here would seem to be identified with Christian believers and the term is buttressed by references to what lies beyond the natural world. When he compares the mystic and the man of common sense it is because paradoxically they have a faculty for the obvious, the one being sure that a donkey has four legs, the other that existence is holy.[34] The latter draws attention to man's religious sense or that innate capacity to perceive that essentially he has a relation to God. We presume that for Chesterton it is because Everyman enjoys that relation, what forbids murder is 'the mystical idea, chiefly the product of Christianity, the idea of the sanctity of an individual life'.[35] For him Christianity is to a large extent 'embodied in the common language talked on the top of an omnibus'.[36] He had the charism of discerning mysteries latent in demotic prose. Nor is it a surprise if laughter enters with uncommon common sense. 'Conviction must always be yoked with humour and humour must be always yoked

30. G. K. Chesterton, *Autobiography*, p. 99.
31. Oddie, *Chesterton and the Romance of Orthodoxy*, p. 254.
32. Ibid., p. 255.
33. Ibid., p. 364.
34. Ibid., p. 259.
35. Ibid.
36. Ibid., p. 281.

with conviction.'[37] This confident optimism was rooted in his faculty of perceiving humanity *sub specie aeternitatis*.

> The man next door is indefinable, because he is too actual to be defined. And there are some to whom spiritual things have the same fierce and practical proximity; some to whom God is too actual to be defined.[38]

This splendid statement raises the question of how God bore in on Chesterton, so to speak. Was it a case of hearsay subjected to his unique intuition or was it through infused contemplation? In a critique of a theology of immanence, Chesterton was reported to have contrasted images of Buddha with those of a medieval saint: 'Buddha had his eyes closed and was looking for God, as it were, in the regions of his soul, while the Christian stared outward to something beyond himself.'[39] This was a way of emphasising the transcendence of God and Christianity's 'dogmatic insistence that God was personal, and had made a world separate from Himself'.[40] What it seems to overlook is that there is a tradition of seeking God within that goes back to the New Testament and finds remarkable expression in the writings of Christian mystics, not least in *The Interior Castle* of St Teresa. Nor does this kind of immanence violate the transcendence emphasised by Chesterton. Encounter and union with God cannot undo the infinite chasm between Creator and creature, but that does not invalidate the orthodoxy of Christian interiorisation. Does this indicate that Chesterton never brought this fact into focus and if so why not? He was exercised by the question of balancing transcendence and immanence and came down on the side of transcendence. The knotty problems that attend the encyclical *Pascendi Dominici Gregis* need not detain us here apart from suggesting that the genuine mystic's union with God never declines into a more or less ill-defined fusion with divinity. If Chesterton knew this from the inside, so to speak, would

[37.] Ibid., p. 267.
[38.] Ibid., p. 314.
[39.] Ibid., pp. 338–9.
[40.] Ibid.

he not have said so or would his massive modesty have forbidden it?

The Irish proverb *aithníonn ciaróg ciaróg eile,* 'it takes one beetle to recognise another', may serve as encouragement to look at Chesterton's books on St Thomas Aquinas and St Francis, not merely to find his use of 'mystic' and its cognates, but also to get some notion of how they resonated with him, and of his affinity with them. Fundamentally, what was significant for him was that both of them imitated Christ: 'when St. Francis walked humbly among the beasts or St Thomas debated courteously among the Gentiles'.[41] Aquinas assured Chesterton that 'A Christian means a man who believes that deity or sanctity has attached to matter or entered the world of the senses.'[42] The Aristotelian rooting of his philosophy in matter and the senses enabled Aquinas to appreciate the theology of the Incarnation in a new way, which overcame a Platonising tendency that had been marked in the preceding centuries. It won renewed respect for the whole realm of the material and challenged the neo-Manichaeism which 'had its roots in the remote mysticism and moral detachment of the East'.[43] Chesterton sees the theology as too much influenced by 'a dried up Platonism'. 'Their Logos was the Word; but not the Word made flesh.' It needed a dose of common sense and Aquinas provided that with Chesterton's unqualified approval. Chesterton finds that in Ghirlandaio's portrait there is 'a smouldering vigilance in his eyes'; his absent-mindedness, 'important in the mystic and philosopher'[44] is that of a man thinking about something, with which he can identify. He does not think that Aquinas's fits of abstraction were those of a Christian mystic. He thinks of them as bemused fits that belong to the 'practical man'. He invokes the distinction between the contemplative life and the active life without defining 'active' as asceticism or activity.[45] He seems to think that

[41.] G. K. Chesterton, *St. Thomas Aquinas,* p. 33.
[42.] Ibid., p. 41.
[43.] Ibid., p. 43.
[44.] Ibid., p. 144.
[45.] Ibid., p. 146.

Aquinas's mind was elsewhere because he was thinking profoundly, not because he was lost in empty reverie and so 'even his contemplative life was an active life', but because he was engaged in the intellectual conflicts of his day. Here Chesterton does not pronounce on 'trances of true Christian mysticism'[46] in the case of Aquinas, but he obviously accepts their happening. If Chesterton is projecting, he is identifying with the man of thought rather than with the man of prayer. He can also identify with him concealing his holiness, 'the one invariable rule'[47] of true sanctity, even if there are variations on the theme.

Having reviewed the Hegelian, the Berkleian, the Pragmatist view of eggs, the author tells us that

> The Thomist stands in the broad daylight of the brotherhood of men, in their common consciousness that eggs are not hens or dreams or mere practical assumptions; but things attested by the Authority of the Senses, which is from God.[48]

It is hard to resist the impression that Chesterton's fellow-feeling for Aquinas is to be found before all else in their common conviction that 'the primary act of recognition of any reality is real'.[49] What it can subsequently deliver was formulated in a perennial philosophy, thought of as *ancilla theologiae*. But Chesterton is sensitive as well to what we can presume is outside his immediate experience. He is respectful of the historicity of events in the life of both Thomas and Francis, something that would not awaken the sympathy of a dogmatic agnostic. He records the mystical girding of the loins of Aquinas and tentatively suggests that it was a kind of 'sublimation; that is the lifting of a lower energy to higher ends'.[50] For Chesterton it is of a piece with what he knows of Aquinas to understand the tradition of a voice from a crucifix asking him what reward he wanted for his work and the saint's answer: 'I will have Thyself.' He characterises the

[46.] Ibid.
[47.] Ibid., p. 157.
[48.] Ibid., p. 177.
[49.] Ibid., p. 175.
[50.] Ibid., p. 157.

answer as one of 'almost blasphemous audacity', paradoxically 'one with the humility of his religion'.[51] Towards the
end of his life we are told that Aquinas had 'a longing for the
inner world which any Catholic can share, and in which the
saint is not cut off from simple men'.[52] We do not have an
elaboration of this, but it is the prelude to an experience,
possibly at Mass, which made Aquinas say to his secretary
Reginald: 'I can write no more. I have seen things which
make all my writings straw.'[53] Chesterton, while acknowl-
edging an inner world and the reality of what is said to have
taken place, is hardly suggesting that mystical phenomena
are the normal lot of 'simple men'.

There is a very interesting passage in *St. Thomas Aquinas*
where Chesterton contrasts St Thomas with St Bonaventure where he says that 'The Franciscan may be represented
as the Father of the Mystics; and the Mystics can be represented as men who maintain that the final fruition or joy of
the soul is rather a sensation than a thought.' Having wittily
contrasted the realisation of 'taste and see' by his two saints,
he shrewdly suggests that

> It might be well maintained that the Franciscan puts taste
> last and the Dominican puts it first. It might be said that the
> Thomist begins with something solid like the taste of an apple,
> and afterwards deduces a divine life for the intellect; while the
> Mystic exhausts the intellect first, and says finally that the sense
> of God is something like the taste of an apple.[54]

While both men were contemplatives, for whom the primacy
of the praise of God was obvious, he thought that Aquinas was
reticent about love while 'mystics and men of the Franciscan
school dwelt on the admitted supremacy of love'.[55] Perhaps
that bothersome term 'sensation', that occurs above, is used
analogously for experiential knowledge of God through

[51.] Ibid., p. 161.
[52.] Ibid., p. 168.
[53.] Ibid.
[54.] Ibid., pp. 82–3.
[55.] Ibid., p. 164.

love. In his study of St Francis of Assisi, he thinks of him as 'the most sublime approximation to his Master', 'a merciful Mirror of Christ'.[56] Chesterton hardly seems to be a likely enthusiast for stigmata and yet in his assessment of what was said to have taken place on Alverno, he is impressed by the attestation of The Three Companions that 'St. Francis received the wounds'.[57] His evocation of the event is quite sublime with its 'mounting agony accompanied by ecstasy' and the contrasting matter-of-factness of its denouement: 'as he stared downwards, he saw the marks of the nails in his own hands'.[58] The most exacting critic would be impressed by Chesterton's realising that the outward signs flowed from an inner identification with the Crucified. What impresses him is that it was integral to Francis' message 'that such mysticism makes a man cheerful and humane'.[59] It was an instance of the paradox that a man becomes more human by having been lifted into another realm, that of grace. When dying, Francis asked to be laid on the bare ground. 'It was the final assertion of his great fixed idea; praise and thanks springing to their most towering height out of nakedness and nothing.'[60] Chesterton undoubtedly had affinity with Thomas and Francis, something that required critical observation, imagination and good judgement. It also required faith, even faith lit up by wisdom. But was it possible to write as he did with these endowments and still remain short of the 'sensation' he noted above?

If there were texts that would indicate mystical gifts in the strict sense in Chesterton, they would surely appear in his poetry. He himself turns to the poetry of Aquinas as evidence of a sensibility that, from the nature of the case, can hardly be conveyed in his prose. For him 'the composer of the Corpus Christi service was not merely what even the wild and woolly would call a poet; he was what the most

[56.] G. K. Chesterton, *St. Francis of Assisi*, London, Hodder and Stoughton Ltd, 1923, p. 134.
[57.] Ibid., p. 165.
[58.] Ibid., p. 152
[59.] Ibid., p. 166.
[60.] Ibid., p. 168.

fastidious would call an artist',[61] a man who could plan on the grand scale and then turn to the microcosm of the lyric. He finds the exultant clash of cymbals in the opening phrase of the *Pange lingua* and rightly asks how anyone could render '*sumit unus, sumunt mille; quantum isti, tantum ille*' in English.[62] He knows that Aquinas has poured his heart into that office and that it is especially revealed in the texture of his poetry. Again his discernment is refined, the work of an acute critic. It does not necessarily mean that he could achieve a comparable poetic expression, not because he could not write poetry, but because he may not have had the *fons et origo* of that kind of verse. T. S. Eliot thought that his poetry was 'first-rate journalistic balladry', while for Marshall McLuhan, who comments on GK's statement that 'All my mental doors open outwards into a world I have not made', considers that 'this distinction must always remain between the artist who is engaged in making a world and the metaphysician who is engaged in contemplating a world'.[63] A contemporary poet and critic, looking at his poetry, finds a general air of melancholy in Chesterton in the face of death and judgement. He thinks that he makes conventional gestures towards God and morality but that these do not come from profound responses, so that they have a lack of persuasiveness.

> He comes into his own – his own distrinctive voice when he indulges in humorous comments – in comedy, social or political observations – and portraits of people. Also he has a sense of history although I think this is normal among educated people. His poetry in comic mode is enjoyable and used to be quoted. He is not a mystic poet. He is more Falstaff than John of the Cross, more cakes and ale than the dark night of the soul. But inspired by a humorous perception of humanity.[64]

[61.] G. K. Chesterton, *St. Thomas Aquinas*, p. 165.

[62.] Ibid., p. 166.

[63.] Oddie, *Chesterton and the Romance of Orthodoxy*, pp. 63–4.

[64.] Professor Maurice Harmon, poet and critic, in an unpublished comment.

Chesterton compared himself to Falstaff, but even if we think that there is more to him than that, it should be instructive to take the hint and put his verse side by side with that of an acknowledged mystical poet, John of the Cross. St John's poem 'The Dark Night of the Soul' has been aptly entitled 'Songs of the soul in rapture at having arrived at the height of perfection, which is union with God by the road of spiritual negation'.[65] John wants us to enter the world of the metaphorical and perhaps to go even further. This poem gives expression to the whole mystical theology of St John. It starts with love and it ends up with love. The poet uses language differently from the rational thinker. His engagement with the world is emotional and he conveys his impressions through aspects of language that go beyond its rational sense, with imagery, rhythm, alliteration, assonance, the music of words. If God cannot be conceptualised and at the same time he makes himself available to our effort to understand him, it is because he can be symbolised.

The poetry of John of the Cross can be seen as the outpouring of symbols in his initial response to the impact of God. The language is symbolic because it brings the nearer and further worlds together and allows us to enter the unknown through the known. The language echoes a 'silent music', a 'clamorous solitude'. Because the experience is located in 'the centre of the soul', the normal location for the mystic poet, his use of language is inverted, referring primarily to his encounter with a divine music and divine solitude and secondarily to that with which his reader can immediately relate. His engagement with the subject of his poetry is emotional and more than emotional. The mystical poet has resonated with a divine disclosure and has the capacity to convey the trace and embers of that experience in a language that evokes the uncreated and created dramatis personae of that encounter. It is emotion charged with the transcendent, which mediates what takes place more inwardly and moulds the language to poetry. There is no definitive way of proving that this is realised in John of the Cross' work and not in that of Chesterton. It comes down to the contrast in

[65.] San Juan de la Cruz, *Obras Completas,* p. 98. My translation.

experience when reading the poetry, and the little Spaniard would seem to have something which we do not necessarily find in the genial Englishman, a *no sé qué* which by common consent is called mysticism.

The suggestion is that the way of the mystic culminates in encounter with God, while that of the thinker finds its term in insight and realisation.

Was Chesterton a Mystic? – 2

Bob Wild

In an unpublished letter, written in 1966, to a priest in England, Etienne Gilson recalls his meeting with Chesterton in Toronto some thirty years earlier. 'Everything which I heard him say,' Gilson writes, 'was an intellectual revelation. With Chesterton, more than literature is at stake. Here, in Toronto, we value him first of all, as a theologian.'[1]

My thesis is that Chesterton's rightness, his not being able to help being right, and the intellectual revelations of his insights were the fruit of a mystical grace.

Mystics do not have 'grandchildren', that is, their graces are not passed on in some organic, hereditary way. Each person, himself or herself, must be open to the new graces from God. The graces which the mystics receive are not communicable as such. God gives genuine mystical graces to whomever he wills, whenever he wills, and however he wills. Ages of crisis, such as ours, are also quite often ages of mysticism, as if God, in his great mercy, keeps the awareness of his Presence alive in times of darkness. However, the spirituality or teaching engendered by powerful mystical experiences can be promoted and serve as inspirations for others, as we see in the various spiritual movements that saintly mystics have spawned in the Church throughout history.

What is a mystic? The Oxford Dictionary says it is someone who has access to spiritual truths beyond the grasp of the ordinary processes of human reasoning and understanding. Chesterton seems to have had these insights into the vast

[1.] Ian Boyd, 'Chesterton: A Prophet for Today', in Christ To the World, *The Chesterton* Review, November 1987, 31.

movements of history and equally into the significance of those apparently trivial events we all experience every day.[2]

My thesis – quite unprovable, although I don't think it can be disproved either – is that Chesterton used this word precisely because he had received some kind of real mystical grace, and that it was out of this personal mystical experience that he spoke. 'Mysticism' was the word which he thought best approximated his own experience, his own vision.

I hope to show that Chesterton was preoccupied with communicating a proper understanding of mysticism, at least in his own terms. If we shall not find in Chesterton a technical theology of mysticism such as we discover in the works of John of the Cross, my contention is that we have in his writings a description of what he called his 'makeshift mystical theory'.[3]

Just to mention John of the Cross is to conjure up notions of terrible trials and dark nights of the soul. No doubt all very great mystics have to undergo awful journeys into the caverns of the spirit. However, I do not think this is necessary in order to receive a particular mystical grace. God can give such a grace to anybody he wants to. Even when we turn to the saints, we find that they are called to various depths of mystical experience, not all equally painful and harrowing.

One rather modern meaning of 'a mystic' is someone who experiences extraordinary phenomena, Bernadette at Lourdes, for example. The Church pronounced on the validity of her visions before declaring her a saint. Chesterton thought William Blake really had some truly mystical visions; I doubt if Chesterton thought he was a saint. In a broad rendering of the term, Clement of Alexandria said that every baptised person is a mystic, precisely because he or she shares in the divine life; but we would not consider every Christian a 'saint' in the Church's canonical sense of the word.

---

2. *The Chesterton Review*, VI, 2, 1986, 206.
3. G. K. Chesterton, *Autobiography*, New York, Sheed and Word, 1936, p. 93.

Some people receive mystical graces which, by the more commonly understood, narrow definition, are extraordinary and not part of the normal journey to God. They may or may not be saints, and oftentimes their graces can be validated apart from their sanctity. Chesterton, I will argue, received such a mystical grace, and it is my purpose to describe it and argue for it. His mystical grace is not bound up with his being a saint, although I believe he was also that. He once said, 'We need a new kind of saint.' I say, 'We need a new kind of mystic,' and this is what Chesterton was.

I hope to show that Chesterton 'fits' into at least some of the traditional definitions of mysticism, and that he is as much a mystic as Plotinus or Tauler or Ruysbroeck. I make special mention of these three men for the sake of comparison precisely because they are not canonised. Indeed, Plotinus was not even a Christian. The Church can approve someone's mystical teaching while leaving open the question of his or her personal sanctity. We have many teachers of mysticism in our tradition who have not been canonised.

When we think of 'mystical graces', our minds turn to St John of the Cross or St Teresa of Avila. These people were Religious in the canonical sense of the word. Nevertheless, because they achieved holiness, many people – laity included – seek to adapt this Carmelite spirituality to their everyday lives in order to achieve holiness.

But for too long lay people have been striving to adopt the mystical spirituality of the cloister or monastery, and have not believed in the authentic paths of lay mysticism which are open to them through the guidance of the Holy Spirit. Chesterton has a clear doctrine of a lay mysticism whose time has come. There are many kinds of mysticism, and Chesterton, for one, has been given the grace of an authentic lay mysticism for the Church.

One of the aspects of Chesterton's life and thought which eventually led me to ask about his mysticism was what might be called his 'charism of truth'. Many observations about Chesterton center around the truth-quality of his mind. In 1986, Cardinal Carter of Toronto, commenting in his homily at the Chesterton Anniversary Conference Mass, mentioned

Chesterton's 'truly prophetic gift'. Writing from England, J. J. Scarisbrick wrote in response of his 'breathtaking, intuitive (almost angelic) possession of the Truth and awareness of the supernatural which only a truly holy person can enjoy' (the full text of Professor Scarisbrick's remarks is quoted on p. 564).

Chesterton's mysticism reveals itself most especially in the realm of the mind. People often know very little about him personally, but they are drawn to him by the depth of his insights. Some of the Church's great minds such as Origen, Augustine and Aquinas have spoken with such depth that the Church has concluded that they were close to God. Would they have been canonised if they had not written those profound things? To be canonised one must have lived the gospel to a heroic degree. Can this heroic virtue be manifested and authenticated through the gospel quality of one's mind? The Church answers yes.

The mystical grace I am arguing for in Chesterton – an immediate awareness of the Presence in and through created reality – affected, of course, his whole person.[4] But it was through the quality of his mind that this grace was principally manifested. In theological terms, it was the gift of knowledge:

> St. Augustine says that according to the distinction which the apostle Paul made when he said, 'to one is given the word of wisdom, to another the word of knowledge' (1 Cor 12:8), we have to discriminate between two different kinds of knowledge: the knowledge of divine things is properly wisdom, and that of human things is properly called knowledge. It is one thing to know only what a man ought to believe in order to attain to a blessed life, which is none other than eternal life, and another to know how this may be of assistance to the pious, and be defended against the wicked, what the apostle seems to mean by 'knowledge'.[5]

[4.] I have written elsewhere of his other virtues such as charity, humility, etc. 'All Things Considered' (former) newsletter of the Ottawa Chesterton Society, 1994, passim.

[5.] Benedict IV, *On the Beatification and Canonization of the Servants of God*, London, Thomas Richardson & Son, 1887, pp. iii, 156.

Chesterton's wife Frances once asked him why he didn't write more about God. He replied, 'I am always writing about God.' But his gift was not that of theological wisdom properly so-called, writing explicitly about the mysteries of the faith. His was the gift of a sort of sacred practical theology, to treat of human affairs in the light of faith. He wrote of St Francis: '[He] cast a new supernatural light on natural things, the ultimate recovery, not refusal, of natural things.' That's exactly the gift Chesterton had through his mystical grace.

This grace of immediacy with the Presence gave a certain definite quality to his thinking. Another kind of grace impels one (Aquinas, for example) to sit down quietly and contemplate the large, eternal plan of things. Chesterton's grace riveted him on present realities, what journalists are interested in:

> I have no feeling for immortality. I don't care for anything except to be in the present stress of life as it is. I would rather live now and die, from an artistic point of view, than keep aloof and write things that will remain in the world hundreds of years after my death.[6]

Mackey comments that in spite of this wish, Chesterton has withstood the test of time extremely well. This 'test of time' is another proof of the profundity of his grace. Although he was immersed in the issues of his day, his insights, we might say, are eternal and have a lasting value. This does not mean, of course, that he was right about everything. But he was right about a great deal, in a way which readers immediately recognise and embrace. Chesterton said that the Church was a '*truth-telling Thing*.' Chesterton was a truth-telling mystic.

Do Mystics Study and Use Their Minds?

There is a disputed question as to the place of study in mysticism which is relevant to our discussion of whether Chesterton was a mystic or not. Don't mystics turn their

6. Quoted by Aidan Mackey in *30 Days*, 'Chesterton, Fidei Defensor', October 1989.

minds off and remain in the darkness of faith? Some do, and some don't. While St Francis saw dangers in the use of the mind, St Thomas saw dangers only in how to use it. Thomas did not doubt that the mind should be used.

It is a matter of debate among the schools of mysticism whether or not learning and study should have a place in the mystical, contemplative life. There is one ancient and strong tradition which says that books, learning, and study are not only not necessary for the deeper life with God, but positively an obstacle. It would be very easy to marshall hundreds of quotations from the Desert Fathers, from the monks of East – especially from the East – and West, and from the writings of some of the mystics, to the effect that learning is an obstacle to the final ascent of the spirit to God. All that is necessary is the Holy Scriptures. For the rest, the mind should be free from the interference of intellectual activity, as it seeks to live entirely by the inspirations of the Holy Spirit:

> As oft I say 'all the creatures that ever be made' are [to be elim-inated], so oft do I mean, not only the creatures themselves, but also all the works and conditions of the same creatures. I except not one creature, whether they be bodily creatures or ghostly; good or evil. But, so speak shortly, all should be hid under the cloud of forgetting in this case.[7]

Although this text does not specifically mention study, the presupposition is that the heights of contemplation do not admit of rational thinking about any creatures. When the mind is in use, contemplation is imperfect.

This question is especially relevant in the case of Chester-ton who, as we know, read voraciously. (He was looking for something on the floor one day, found a book, and stayed there and read it.) How can Chesterton be a mystic if he didn't stop his mind and enter the Cloud of Unknowing?

However, there is definitely another tradition – Irenaeus, Justin, Origin, the Cappadocians, Augustine, Jerome, Maximus the Confessor, Aquinas, Anselm and countless other Fathers – many or most of whom were certainly

---

7. Dom Justin McCann (ed.), *The Cloud of Unknowing*, London, Burns & Oates, 1943, ch. 5, p. 11.

mystics. They evidently hadn't heard of this problem, since they had no difficulty with the intellectual life as such. For them it was a matter of how to use the mind, not whether or not to use it. Their libraries were often enormous, and study did not lessen their union with God. They believed, of course, that all knowledge had to be subject to the light of Christ ('all truth comes from the Holy Spirit' was a common patristic saying), but they did not see knowledge per se as hindering the mystical life.

Chesterton has a brief section on this subject in *St. Francis*. As is well known, St Francis was not all that enthusiastic about books. He himself wrote: 'Let the illiterate not worry about learning to read, but consider that above all things they should desire to have the spirit of the Lord and its holy working.'[8] Nimmo's studied conclusion is this:

> The truth would seem to be that, although not categorically opposed to learned study by the friars, he had the gravest reservations about it, for the good reason that it was a threat to all four prime characteristics of Franciscan life – poverty, humility, simplicity, the spirit of devotion. (Ibid.)

It is interesting to see how Chesterton handles this topic in relation to Francis. Basically he says that Francis was unique, and that as the one who stands at the origin of the medieval age, it was not necessary for him to know what went before:

> There is not a trace in the poetry of this first Italian poet of all that pagan mythology which lingered after paganism. The first Italian poet seems the only man in the world who has never even heard of Virgil. This was exactly right for the special sense in which he is the first Italian poet. It is the essence of the story that he should pluck at the green grass without knowing it grows over a murdered man or climb the apple tree without knowing it was the gibbet of a suicide. It was such an amnesty and reconciliation that the freshness of the Franciscan brought to all the world.[9]

8. Duncan Nimmo, *Reform and Division in the Medieval Franciscan Order (1226–1538)*, Rome, Capuchin Historical Institute, 1987, p. 22.
9. G. K. Chesterton, *St. Francis*, New York, Sheed & Ward, 1924, pp. 225–6.

But Chesterton is very grateful that the Fratricelli, who would have turned this grace of Francis into a principle, did not prevail. He is glad Dante knew of Virgil; glad, too, that the Franciscans produced Bonaventure, Raymond Lull, Roger Bacon, and Duns Scotus.

> It is not merely true that these were great men who did great work for the world; it is also true that they were a certain kind of men keeping the spirit and savour of a certain kind of man, that we can recognise in them a taste and tang of audacity and simplicity, and know them for the sons of St. Francis.[10]

Chesterton's voracious appetite for knowledge. therefore, is not opposed to authentic mysticism: his vocation required it. He had the gift of knowledge, which precisely is reflection on the practical aspects of life in order to illumine them with the light of faith. One needs open eyes for this task. He did not see the things of earth as distracting him from a mystical vision of the Presence. His experience of the Presence was mediated precisely through the stimuli which the five windows of his nature could afford him.

Similarly, he experienced the Presence, as did St Thomas, in the truths his mind was able to assimilate, for God is Truth as well as Love. It follows that, if God is Truth, when your mind knows truth, you are also, in some real sense, touching God, the First Truth. In the same way, if you love, you touch God, seeing as God is Love.

It was this 'First Truth' who spoke to St Catherine of Siena in her Treatise on Divine Providence. Passages frequently open thus: 'The First Truth showed her; then the Eternal Truth seized and drew more strongly to Himself her desire; the Sweet Truth continued.' In another passage she explains: 'He used to say: "Open the eye of thy intellect, and gaze into Me, and thou shalt see the beauty of My rational creature."'[11] Coming, as it does, from one of the great mystics of the Middle Ages, this is an inspired corroboration of an

[10.] Ibid., p. 230.
[11.] Catherine of Siena, *The Dialogue*, tr. Suzanne Noffke, New York, Paulist Press, 1980, pp. 202–4.

attitude towards the life of the mind which many learned
Christian Fathers and teachers had.

St Thomas: 'Taste and See'

Thomas Aquinas – the mystical mind – completes Chesterton's Christian understanding of mysticism.

It is hard to say exactly when Chesterton first heard of
Aquinas (there is a reference to him in *Heretics*), or really
seriously studied him. We do, however, know that his brilliant, book-length study of Saint Thomas Aquinas[12] appeared
late in his life, three years before his death in 1936. Nor is it
easy to say where or when he conceived his exalted notion
of Aristotle, whom he called the wisest and greatest mind
that ever existed (cf. *The Everlasting Man*). Whatever the
case, in both Thomas Aquinas and Aristotle he found the
philosophical position which explained his own mystical
intuition of Being. Aquinas is the philosopher of *ens*, of the
it-is-thereness of being. And Chesterton is the mystic of the
goodness of whatever is. The Presence was manifested most
of all in the goodness of the good things the good God had
made.

In the chapter in *St. Thomas* entitled 'The Aristotelian
Revolution', Chesterton has the following description of St
Bonaventure, the great Franciscan theologian of the Middle
Ages:

> The Franciscan may be represented as the Father of all the
> Mystics; and the Mystics can be represented as men who
> maintain that the final fruition or joy of the soul is rather a
> sensation than a thought. The motto of the Mystics has always
> been, 'Taste and see.' (p. 73)

In mentioning 'final fruition' Chesterton is referring briefly
to the interminable question of which has ultimate finality,
love or knowledge. The question is not of immediate
concern to us here, although it must be said that Chesterton does come down gently on the side of knowledge: 'The

[12.] G. K. Chesterton, *St. Thomas Aquinas*, London, Hodder & Stoughton,
1933. Page references refer to this edition unless otherwise noted.

appetite for truth may outlast and even devour all the duller appetites of man' (p. 74). My main concern is this other statement that occurs in the same context, where Chesterton compares St Thomas, the Dominican, with St Bonaventure, the Franciscan:

> The motto of the Mystics has always been, 'Taste and see.' Now St. Thomas also began by saying, 'Taste and see'; but he said it of the first rudimentary impressions of the human animal. It might well be maintained that the Franciscan puts taste last and the Dominican puts it first. It might be said that the Thomist begins with something solid like the taste of an apple, and afterwards deduces a divine life for the intellect; while the Mystic exhausts the intellect first, and says finally that the sense of God is something like the taste of an apple. (p. 73)

What does Chesterton mean here, when he refers to Bonaventure as a mystic, in seeming contrast to Thomas? Indeed he calls Bonaventure the 'Father of all the mystics'. I'm sure he considered Thomas a mystic no less than he did Bonaventure and his followers. When he uses the term 'mystics' here, he is speaking about the more broadly accepted definition of mysticism, about people who devise elaborate theories about the Presence behind sensible reality. In this vein, for example, many consider Plato a genuine mystic. These theorists can generally be called 'intellectual mystics', who 'exhaust the intellect' in profound speculations about the nature of things, and then conclude that the sense of God – the Presence – has 'tastes' or 'vestiges' in our tangible world. Aquinas, as well as Chesterton, who banged his head on a post, contend that human consciousness begins with the taste of the intuition of being:

> St. Thomas says emphatically that the child is aware of Ens. Long before he knows that grass is grass, or self is self, he knows that something is something. Perhaps it would be best to say very emphatically (with a blow on the table), 'There is an Is.' That is as much monkish credulity as St. Thomas asks of us to believe at the start. (p. 166)

Thomas and Chesterton begin their journey with the extraor-
dinariness of *ens* itself. They believe we first 'taste', with the
totality of our faculties, the elementary existence of things,
and 'see' afterwards. Their mysticism is not a reposing 'in
the peace of timeless being', in the interior vision, but in
the actual tasting of reality, the 'it-is-thereness' of the good
creation.

In summing up the essence of Thomism, Chesterton says
that Aquinas is arguing for the popular proverbs that seeing
is believing; that the proof of the pudding is in the eating;
that a man cannot jump down his own throat or deny the
fact of his own existence (p. 156).

We have seen that another tag Chesterton uses for mystics
who are more fascinated by the inner world they construct
than by the amazing world they can see is *mere mystic*:

> 'Every thing that is in the intellect has been in the senses.'
> This is where he began at the opposite end of enquiry from
> that of the mere mystic. The Platonists, or at least the Neo-
> Platonists, all tended to the view that the mind was lit entirely
> from within; St. Thomas insisted that it was lit by five windows,
> that we call the windows of the senses. But he wanted the light
> from without to shine on what was within. (ch. 7, p. 161)

> Man is not a balloon going up into the sky, nor a mole burrow-
> ing merely in the earth; but rather a thing like a tree, whose
> roots are fed from the earth, while its highest branches seem to
> rise almost to the stars. (p. 164)

The last paragraph of the chapter entitled, 'The Permanent
Philosophy', tries to sum up St Thomas. It is also as succinct
a statement of the philosophy undergirding Chesterton's
own mysticism as you will find anywhere. As spirit in matter,
we have an insatiable longing for pure beauty, pure being,
pure truth. Yet, here we are in this land of shadows and
change and limitations. (For his epitaph Cardinal Newman
chose *Ex Umbris in Veritatem*.) What we see is real being,
only it is not, as Chesterton said, all it could be.

Because of this tension between the 'limited seen' and
the 'infinite unseen', we both underestimate and under-
value what we do see. We think, moreover, that we know

more than we do about what we can't see. And what we can't see becomes more fascinating than what we can see. Of the all too many decadent scholastics, Chesterton said: 'The world was cumbered with countless tomes, proving by logic a thousand things that can be known only to God.' I think he would say the same about many 'mere mystics'. Here is his final statement:

> The deceitfulness of things which has had so sad an effect on so many sages, has almost a contrary effect on this sage [Thomas]. If things deceive us, it is by being more real than they seem. As ends in themselves they always deceive us; but as things tending to a greater end, they are even more real than we think them. If they seem to have a relative unreality (so to speak) it is because they are potential and not actual; they are unfulfilled, like packets of seeds or boxes of fireworks. They have it in them to be more real than they are. (p. 18)

Because of his mystical intuition of the goodness of what he could see with his eyes, Chesterton was content to wait for the fireworks of eternity. Meanwhile, he did not want to miss this world in some kind of premature anticipation of the next. He knew that what he saw with his eyes was not all that he could reason to with his mind. But he found the actual goodness more captivating than an imagined or rational construct of the mind.

This is perfectly in keeping with his whole mysticism: penetration and insight into the present were more real for him than constructing an abstract theory about how the whole universe fits together and runs. His mysticism illuminates things as they are; he does not give us theories to help us abstract from what we can see, although he does acknowledge an ultimate manifestation of the structure of reality:

> And there is an upper world of what the Schoolman called Fruition, or Fulfilment, in which all this relative relativity becomes actuality; in which the trees burst into flower or the rockets into flame. (p. 180)

For Chesterton – at least in this present life – the light from without was more brilliant than the light within. He did not wish to go up into the sky in a balloon before his time. The highest branches of his tree did almost reach the stars anyhow. He would rather wait for the real flowers, see the actual explosions, than try to picture them in his mind.

> The mind conquers a new province like an emperor; but only because the mind has answered the bell like a servant. The mind has opened the doors and windows, because it is the natural activity of what is inside the house to find out what is outside the house. If the mind is sufficient to itself, it is insufficient for itself. For this feeding upon fact is itself; as an organ it has an object which is objective; this eating of the strange meat of reality. (p. 184)

One of my favourite passages from Chesterton, and one which describes his own inner mind working on the stuff of creation, comes from *St. Thomas*. Chesterton is describing the saint's closing hours, and speaks of those standing around his bed:

> They must have felt that, for that moment, the inside of the monastery was larger than the outside. It must have resembled the case of some mighty modern engine, shaking the ramshackle building in which it is for the moment enclosed. For truly that machine was made of the wheels of all the worlds; and revolved like that cosmos of concentric spheres which, whatever its fate in the face of changing science, must always be something of a symbol for philosophy; the depth of double and triple transparencies more mysterious than darkness; the seven fold, the terrible crystal. In the world of that mind there was a wheel of angels, and a wheel of planets, and a wheel of plants or of animals; but there was also a just and intelligible order of all earthly things, a sane authority and a self-respecting liberty, and a hundred answers to a hundred questions in the complexity of ethics or economics. But there must have been a moment, when men knew that the thunderous mill of thought had stopped suddenly ...[13]

Chesterton's mysticism included his own 'thunderous mill of thought'. The Presence was mediated to him through

[13.] G. K. Chesterton, *St Thomas Aquinas*, p. 205.

all the lovely things God had made. The only mirror Chesterton didn't mind was the reflection of the truth of reality in his intellect, where, as Eternal Truth said to Catherine of Siena, he could gaze on the beauty of the Creator's creatures.

Chesterton:
The Journalist as Saint

Sheridan Gilley

In Chesterton's beloved Middle Ages, it was customary that
trades and professions should have a patron saint. This
sometimes had reference to the manner of his martyrdom,
as St Bartholomew was the patron of tanners, and I like to
think, of the thin-skinned, but it maintained the idea that
there is an ideal human type for everyone and everything,
a little Christ below Christ himself. This figure has often, in
part at least, been an exemplar and a critic and correction
to the sins of the profession. Of course not all saints are
intended as holy exemplars: some have converted nations,
performed miracles, practised a ferocious asceticism,
founded religious Orders, been great theologians or been
martyred, or functioned posthumously as local or national
patrons and heroes.[1] Many saints are, as they say, for edi-
fication, not imitation, with a power deriving from their
very peculiarity, such as those early martyrs whose cultus in
the late Middle Ages was founded in a virginity which their
devotees had no need to share.

---

[1] On the sheer range of functions performed by saints, see, for example,
Stephen Wilson (ed.), *Saints and their Cults: Studies in Religious Soci-
ology, Folklore and History*, Cambridge, Cambridge University Press,
1983; Graham Jones, *Saints in the Landscape*, Stroud, Tempus, 2007.
They exist in the Moslem, Hindu and Buddhist traditions as well as
the Christian, and are related to devotions to the non-human angels
and even to inanimate objects like relics. I have tried to summarise the
Roman Catholic view in 'Holiness in the Roman Catholic Tradition',
Stephen C. Barton (ed.), *Holiness Past and Present*, London, T. & T.
Clark, 2003, pp. 316–38.

There is a further difficulty with the professional exemplar, that some professions might seem beyond salvation. There was a question allegedly debated in the medieval schools: 'Can an Archdeacon be saved?' and banking, politics, and estate agents might seem to be in similar case; but bankers have St Matthew, and politicians St Thomas More. For estate agents, I can only think of Judas Iscariot and the field of blood. The difficulty of the low professional standard is noted by the hymn in honour of the thirteenth-century Breton St Ives, the patron saint of lawyers:

> *Sanctus Ivo erat Brito,*
> *Advocatus et non latro,*
> *Res miranda populo.* [2]
> Ives was a Breton,
> A lawyer and not a thief,
> A wonder to the people.

The patron saint of Catholic writers is St Francis de Sales, so declared in 1923,[3] a writer and a delightful man, but as a seventeenth-century bishop, he lacks the representative character of having been a modern journalist himself. Chesterton, on the other hand, was an example and a correction to his profession, to a degree suggesting heroic sanctity. The suggestion of canonising Chesterton seems to have come originally from the Tudor historian Professor J. J. Scarisbrick in a letter in the November 1986 issue of the *The Chesterton Review*,[4] which also contained a homily on Chesterton by Cardinal Carter of Toronto, at a fiftieth anniversary Mass in his memory. It was in response that Peter J. Floriani subsequently published the propers of a suggested Mass in his honour.[5] I should add that I first heard his cause seriously suggested, not in England, but in a Chesterton conference in 2005 in Buenos Aires, in Argentina, where his reputation is partly due to the translations of his works by Jorge Luis

---

[2.] 'Ives (Yves)', *The Catholic Encyclopedia*, 15 vols, New York, The Encyclopedia Press, 1913, vol. VIII, p. 256.

[3.] F. L. Cross (ed.), *The Oxford Dictionary of the Christian Church*, 3rd edn by E. A. Livingstone, Oxford, Oxford University Press, 1997, p. 634.

[4.] *The Chesterton Review*, vol. XII, no 4, November 1986, p. 564.

[5.] Ibid., vol. XIV, no. 4, November 1988, pp. 641–4.

Borges. Five hundred people attended the opening session of the conference in the Catholic University. Two cardinals presided at the Masses in his honour, and wine was supplied to the gathering by a local vineyard. The editor of the chief newspaper of the city received the conference delegation, and the event was trumpeted in his paper.

This was not inappropriate. Chesterton regarded himself as chiefly 'a jolly journalist': he was not primarily a novelist or a poet or an essayist – though he was also all those things – but a man who earned his living from writing for and editing newspapers. His wife tried to rescue him from a life among editors, presses and printers in London by removing him in 1909 to the rural quiet of Beaconsfield, and some have criticised the misplacement of his creative energies – which should have been given to producing books – on editing the small-circulation periodicals the *New Witness* and *G. K.'s Weekly*, or scribbling the essays which over thirty-one years appeared in almost every edition of the weekly *Illustrated London News*. Of some of the journalism of Chesterton's last decade, A. L. Maycock wrote, 'What waste of time and effort for a mind like his!'[6] But many of Chesterton's books grew out of journal articles or stories which appeared first in newspapers, such as all the volumes of essays and his two works on Ireland, *Irish Impressions* and *Christendom in Dublin*. He operated here on the sound commercial principle that what had sold once would sell again; his medium was print, but newsprint most of all.

Thus like any journalist, Chesterton wrote for the occasion. He has an hilarious essay on the way in which the combination of the journalist's procrastination and the newspaper

---

6. *The Man who was Orthodox: A Selection from the Uncollected Writings of G. K. Chesterton.* Arranged and introduced by A. L. Maycock, London, Dennis Dobson, 1963, p. 34. Maycock's 'Introduction' to this work is the foundational essay on Chesterton as a journalist. See, however, the excellent critique by John Coates, 'The Journalistic Arena', in *Chesterton and the Edwardian Cultural Crisis*, Hull, Hull University Press, 1984, pp. 46–84; and James V. Schall, 'G. K. Chesterton, Journalist', in *Schall on Chesterton: Timely Essays on Timeless Paradoxes*, Washington, The Catholic University of America Press, 2000, p. 13.

deadline results in a catalogue of errors,[7] and another on how the 'blind idolatry of speed' makes it impossible for newspapers to find the truth.[8] Yet 'I could be a journalist because I could not help being a controversialist',[9] he wrote, and his sanctity lies, not least, in his gift for controversy. Thus his best comic or satiric verses were inspired by immediate causes, such as the immortal 'Antichrist, or the Reunion of Christendom: An Ode', beginning 'Are they clinging to their crosses, F. E. Smith', ridiculing an unlucky piece of hyperbole by the future Earl of Birkenhead which enabled Chesterton to extract the humour from the unlikely subject of the Welsh Church Disestablishment Bill.[10] Smith had ventured rashly into an area on which he could hardly claim authority, 'the souls of Christian peoples', and here as elsewhere, it was Chesterton's special gift to throw a devastating squib at a passing piece of pomposity. The chapter in his apologia, *Orthodoxy*, entitled 'The Ethics of Elfland' had one origin in his attack in the *Illustrated London News* on the Duchess of Somerset for urging the abolition of teaching fairy tales in schools, when Chesterton thought that these tales offered a profounder imaginative truth than ordinary history.[11]

Chesterton's early works like *Heretics* and *Orthodoxy* are deeply rooted in the journalistic culture of their time, having their origins in his joustings with other popular writers in newspapers, some of them considerable figures like H. G. Wells and George Bernard Shaw, but most of them, such as the anti-Catholic Joseph McCabe or Robert Blatchford, editor of the Socialist journal *The Clarion*, or G. S. Street, who occasioned the writing of *Orthodoxy*, are now one with Nineveh and Tyre, as lost as Lyonnesse beneath the sea.

---

7. 'The Real Journalist', in Dorothy Collins (ed.), *A Miscellany of Men by G. K. Chesterton*, Beaconsfield, Darwen Finlayson, 1969, pp. 66–70.

8. Cited Schall, *Chesterton*, p. 16.

9. G. K. Chesterton, *Autobiography*, London, Hutchinson, 1937, p. 289.

10. *The Collected Poems of G. K. Chesterton*, London, Methuen, 1933, pp. 152–4.

11. 'Education by Fairy Tales', from the *Illustrated London News*, vol. XXVII, 2 December 1905. See also 'Fairy Tales' in *All Things Considered*, London, Methuen, 1908: edn of 1928, pp. 188–92.

The reputations of most journalists, then, die with their generation, like summer flowers, but the idea of the mere journalist, the commentator or celebrant of ephemera, vastly underestimates their importance in the modern world. Chesterton's life – his dates are 1874–1936 – coincided with the rise of the English press to its role as the so-called Fourth Estate, a phrase attributed by Thomas Carlyle to Edmund Burke but probably Victorian in origin, and to a position of cultural predominance in English life. Chesterton's own life-time was the age of the Yellow Press, a term first applied in 1895 to the *New York World* from its cartoon depicting 'The Yellow Kid', a child in yellow costume, which was at first an experiment in colour printing, but which came to symbolise the paper's lurid contents.[12] Thus the 1890s saw the emergence of the first 'press barons' of this new and murky realm, the great newspaper proprietors, the Irish Harmsworth brothers (who became Viscount Northcliffe and Viscount Rothermere), who together created the *Daily Mail* and bought *The Times*, and later, of the Canadian Baron Beaverbrook, owner of the *Daily Express*, who was so deliciously denounced with Rothermere by the Conservative politician Stanley Baldwin, in Kipling's words, as aiming at 'power without responsibility – the prerogative of the harlot throughout the ages'.[13] Their megalomaniac ruthlessness reached a peak of notoriety in the United States with William Randolph Hearst. The leading satirists made mock of them in the persons of their great fictional equivalents. These include John Buchan's Thomas Carlyle Craw, who 'exposed abuses with a trenchant pen when his lawyers had convinced him that he was on safe legal ground'; whose newspapers specialised in syrupy platitudes, whose power was immense, but whose life was dominated by the fear of being embarrassed by his journalistic rivals, to the point of declining the usual peerage.[14] There are also Evelyn Waugh's Lord Monomark

---

[12.] *Oxford English Dictionary,* Oxford, Oxford University Press.

[13.] *Chambers Dictionary of Quotations,* London, Chambers, 1996, pp. 64–5.

[14.] In *Castle Gay,* original edn, 1930, republished in *The Adventures of Dickson McCunn,* London, Hodder & Stoughton, 1937, p. 329.

of the *Daily Excess* in *Vile Bodies*, who bears a close resemblance to Lord Beaverbrook; Lord Copper of *Scoop*, with whom his minions can only disagree, by agreeing with him up to point; and P. G. Wodehouse's Lord Tilbury of the Mammoth Publishing Company, whose chief aim is the publication of an embarrassing memoir which is, appropriately, eaten by a pig.[15] In Evelyn Waugh's words in 1938, written during the composition of *Scoop*, mingling fastidiousness with snobbery, 'the daily press has sunk to a condition when it is a profession not only unsuitable to a gentleman but to an Englishman ...'[16]

Yet these were the new lords of humankind. As another journalist and writer of genius, Rudyard Kipling, declared in his verses 'The Press', which conclude his account of 'The Village that Voted the Earth was Flat':

> The Pope may launch his Interdict,
>   The Union its decree,
> But the bubble is blown and the bubble is pricked
>   By Us and such as We.
> Remember the battle and stand aside
>   While Thrones and Powers confess
> That King over all the children of pride
>   Is the Press – the Press – the Press![17]

The press seemed to hold the highest power in the land. As Chesterton's friend Hilaire Belloc wrote of Lord Lundy:

> We had intended you to be
> The next Prime Minister but three:
> The stocks were sold; the Press was squared;
> The Middle Class was quite prepared.[18]

[15] P. G. Wodehouse, *Heavy Weather*, London, Hutchinson, 1933.

[16] Cited Martin Stannard, *Evelyn Waugh: The Early Years* 1903–1939, London, J. M. Dent & Sons, 1986, p. 473.

[17] Rudyard Kipling, 'The Press', in *A Diversity of Creatures*, 1st edn, 1917; London, Macmillan, 1966, p. 215.

[18] 'Lord Lundy', Hilaire Belloc, *Complete Verse*, London, Gerald Duckworth, 1970, p. 207.

'Squaring the Press' had replaced the old monarchic device of tuning the pulpits, of telling the public what to think through their priests, and had become one of the great black arts of the new democratic age.

Chesterton called the Yellow Press the 'drab press',[19] partly for its unwillingness either to indulge in a proper sensationalism, which he enjoyed, the healthy sensationalism of the detective story or of the old crime novels called 'penny dreadfuls', or to attack the real injustices of life or abuse of power. Of Northcliffe, Chesterton wrote that he 'bought a pulpit from which ideas could have been given, when he had no ideas to give'.[20] He thought the chief characteristic of the 'Yellow Press', in John Coates's words, was 'a hypnotic beat of stale commonplace repetition', Northcliffe himself being 'by nature ignorant of the very idea of an idea'.[21] Chesterton called the typical writer for the Harmsworth Press 'a man who writes things on the back of advertisements',[22] or in the self-satisfied words of an editor of *The Times* to the sometime journalist John Morley, 'You left journalism a profession; we have made it a branch of commerce.'[23] Chesterton notes in his *Autobiography* that a newspaper proprietor had said to him that 'A newspaper office is now exactly like any other place of business', and that he had agreed with a groan. 'It is conducted as quietly, as soberly, as sensibly', he wrote, 'as the office of any successful moneylender or moderately fraudulent financier', and partook of the profit-and-loss cut-throat character of capitalism itself. [24]

Indeed Chesterton's very style, its verbal brilliancy, its

[19] G. K. Chesterton, 'The Mildness of the Yellow Press', in *Heretics*, London, John Lane, The Bodley Head, 1905: edn of 1919, p. 114.

[20] 'Alfred Harmsworth' (a review of R. Macnair Wilson, *Lord Northcliffe: A Study*), in *The Chesterton Review*, vol. XXIX, no. 4, winter 2003, p. 486.

[21] Coates, p. 55, also quoting Chesterton in *The Man who was Orthodox*, p. 137.

[22] Cited *The Man who was Orthodox*, p. 15.

[23] Ibid., p. 23.

[24] G. K. Chesterton, *Autobiography*, pp. 185–6.

evocation of the strangeness of things, its love of paradox, its genius for metaphor, was directed at the flabbiness of contemporary journalistic prose and its substitution for the awe and wonder of the cosmos of a false flat view of the external world. Yet Chesterton thought that ideally, a journalist who by the very nature of his craft deals with the everyday, ought to discern how extraordinary it is. The journalist should by his ordinary activities have the gift of extracting the magical from the commonplace. For Chesterton, a thing had to be seen with the imagination to be truly seen; it had to be vivid to be true. He was trained as an artist, and had an artist's eye for colour; you could say for technicolour as well.

Chesterton believed that this underlies the truth of religion. The Enlightenment had found the universal claims of Christianity dubious because it was given at a particular time and place to a particular people and through a particular Person. Chesterton, reared in the high-sounding vagueness of liberal Unitarianism, the heir to Platonism and Germanic idealism, thought that Christianity was proven by its particularity, as a story. He once wrote in a child's picture book:

> Stand up and keep childishness;
>   Read all the pedants' screeds and strictures:
> But don't believe in anything
>   That can't be told in coloured pictures.[25]

The resort to abstraction was a mark of journalistic dishonesty. Chesterton's portrait of his fictional editor Edward Nutt, of the *Daily Reformer*, in the Father Brown story 'The Purple Wig', is too unkind to have been based directly on his own indulgent editor, A. G. Gardiner, at the *Daily News*, but it depicts this determination of the great press lords not to disturb the reading public, by feeding them on an anodyne prose which replaces the individual term with the general one. Thus Nutt automatically substitutes the colourless word for the concrete and colourful one in the copy before him: 'adultery' becomes 'impropriety', 'shoot down'

[25.] 'An Inscription in a Child's Picture Book', *The Chesterton Review*, vol. XXVI, nos 1 and 2, February and May, 2000, p. 9.

becomes 'repress', while 'supernatural' is secularised as 'marvellous' and 'God' as 'circumstances'.[26]

There was good journalistic reason for this caution: Nutt, as Chesterton describes him, lived in a state of 'continuous fear: fear of libel actions, fear of lost advertisements, fear of misprints, fear of the sack'. His life was 'a series of distracted compromises' between his staff and his proprietor, 'a senile soap-boiler with three ineradicable mistakes in his mind' for whom the news had to be managed in his political party's interest and to win him a title.[27] The reference to the 'senile soap-boiler' was probably a hit at the soap manufacturer Sir William Lever, who threatened Chesterton with a libel action for describing his model workers' town of Port Sunlight as 'corresponding to a Slave Compound'.[28] The Levers were excellent employers by the standards of the time, but their employees, though cosseted, were denied such basic English freedoms as an inn or public house in which to drink beer. Chesterton saw the right to get drunk as a primary liberty. Like the Victorian Archbishop Magee, he preferred England free to England sober. Some of his best poems are drinking songs. He found the Levers' sort of teetotal paternalism, embodied in the coldly Nietzschean character of Lord Ivywood in *The Flying Inn,* who wants to abolish alcohol in England, as more pernicious than a harsh and exploitative factory regime which made no such pretence to benevolence.

The great newspaper proprietors have become even more powerful, prominent and unpleasant in our own day, such as the Australian-born Rupert Murdoch, wooed and feted by major politicians, and any consideration of the character of English culture must now treat what is peddled in newspapers and magazines, and their bastard children in radio and television. The popular press is even more a kind of opiate than it was in Chesterton's time, being

---

26. 'The Purple Wig', in G. K. Chesterton, *The Father Brown Stories,* London, Cassell, 1969, pp. 244–55.
27. G. K. Chesterton, 'The Purple Wig', p. 245.
28. Maisie Ward, *Gilbert Keith Chesterton,* London, Sheed & Ward, 1944, p. 319.

devoted almost entirely to entertainment and to the cultus of sportsmen, film stars and other 'celebrities'. The quality newspapers have a certain social status and power, but this is still, as Baldwin said, power without responsibility. A large part of the Church's problem in modern Britain is that high culture, both in print and on film, is dominated by a metropolitan elite of journalists hostile to Christianity. It is remarkable how far the British intellectual classes, so-called, are influenced by the modern princes of the press, the columnists on the principal middle-class dailies, so that what Polly Toynbee writes about religion in *The Guardian*, or Matthew Parris in *The Times*, though based on ignorance and prejudice is taken with proper seriousness. In short, to modify Shelley, journalists rather than poets are now the legislators of mankind, though they cannot be called unac-knowledged ones.

There is a paradox here: that in spite of their influence, and the general lowering of the esteem in which British society now holds doctors, lawyers and priests – all have been the subject of recent scandals – journalists have a very low rating in national surveys of the prestige of the pro-fessions, ranking somewhere at the bottom of the social hierarchy of public respect, with the aforenamed estate agents and politicians. The satirical magazine *Private Eye* calls its fellow-journalists reptiles. It calls Fleet Street the 'Street of Shame', Fleet Street being still a way of referring to the press, as in Chesterton's lifetime it was the place in London where national newspapers were printed and pub-lished. Recent attacks on the calling include J. K. Rowling's portrait of the slimy and devious Rita Skeeter. The common view of the journalist as 'hired hack' –'hack' is now chiefly a synonym for pressman – was summed up in 1930 by one of Chesterton's near contemporaries, Humbert Wolfe:

> You cannot hope
> To bribe or twist,
> thank God! the
> British journalist.

> But, seeing what
> the man will do,
> unbribed, there's
> no occasion to.[29]

Chesterton put it just as bluntly in 1909:

> It is by this time practically impossible to get the truth out of
> any newspaper, even the honest newspapers ... I mean the
> kind of truth that a man can feel an intelligent curiosity about
> – moral truth, truth that is disputed, truth that is in action and
> really affecting things.[30]

Where Wolfe seemed to blame the journalists for this, Chesterton chiefly blames their employers. As early as 1905, he
wrote in *Heretics* 'that for purposes of real public opinion
the press is now a mere plutocratic oligarchy' controlled
by rich men.[31] In a celebrated poem, 'When I came back to
Fleet Street', he called his fellow-journalists the 'Prisoners
of the Fleet', in an allusion to the former Fleet Prison, which
was once used to house debtors, and had imprisoned Mr
Pickwick. Chesterton describes its journalists as prisoners
held there by their employers to do their will, as no better
than slaves who wrote what they were told to write from
their need for a crust:

> But old things held; the laughter,
>   The long unnatural night,
> And all the truth they talk in hell,
>   And all the lies they write.
>
>   ...

[29.] *The Oxford Dictionary of Modern Quotations*, Oxford, Oxford University Press, 2002, p. 343.
[30.] Cited Schall, *Chesterton*, p. 13.
[31.] G. K. Chesterton, 'The Mildness of the Yellow Press', *Heretics*, p. 127.

They did not break the padlocks,
  Or clear the wall away.
The men in debt that drank of old
Still drink in debt today;
Chained to the rich by ruin,
Cheerful in chains, as then
When old unbroken Pickwick walked
Among the broken men.[32]

Yet Chesterton's affection for journalists, 'the broken men', the characters of his youth who were eccentric but honest, was as real as his contempt, and it has been richly rewarded; he is still a great man to his fellow-journalists. In this, there is a tremendous contrast between his popular and academic reputations. As the senior partner of Macmillan reading his book on Browning discovered, he lacked the scholarly temperament of accuracy in small things, and could never be bothered to check his dates or quotations. His writings stand nowhere in academia: there are very few university courses which study him. He usually despised professors as narrow specialists and guardians of an elite tradition, who discounted the opinions of the people; the academic always makes the correction and misses the point:

The sages have a hundred maps to give
That trace their crawling cosmos like a tree,
They rattle reason out through many a sieve
That stores the sand and lets the gold go free;
And all these things are less than dust to me
Because my name is Lazarus and I live.[33]

For Chesterton, as for the man on the street, there was a contradiction between scholarship and life. Chesterton's scorn of professors has been repaid in the universities, if not in kind, by ignorance and indifference. But an Internet search of recent British newspaper references to him shows

[32.] G. K. Chesterton, 'When I came back to Fleet Street', *Collected Poems*, pp. 185–6.
[33.] G. K. Chesterton, 'The Convert', *Collected Poems*, p. 387.

that he is still widely quoted, and that it is his fellow journalists who quote him and honour his memory.

His conviction, however, that the journalism of the day was in conflict with the truth, had its origin in his disillusionment with his own early newspaper the *Daily News* and its owner George Cadbury, the Quaker chocolate and cocoa manufacturer, the prince of the so-called 'Cocoa press', and the high priest of the liberalism of Chesterton's own young manhood. Chesterton's Socialist friend George Bernard Shaw once referred to him as 'a flourishing property of Mr Cadbury',[34] but Chesterton was increasingly distressed with Cadbury's liberalism, a liberalism which he saw as a cause of corruption and a financial ramp for the exploitation of the poor, in a conspiracy of which the press was now a part. As the maker of cocoa, Cadbury was the villain of one of Chesterton's poems, 'The Song of Strange Drinks', later retitled 'The Song of Right and Wrong'

> Tea, although an Oriental,
> Is a gentleman at least;
> Cocoa is a cad and coward,
> Cocoa is a vulgar beast,
> Cocoa is a dull, disloyal,
> Lying, crawling cad and clown,
> And may very well be grateful
> To the fool that takes him down.[35]

After the verses on cocoa, published in the *New Witness* on 23 January 1913, Chesterton was dismissed by A. G. Gardiner from the *Daily News* and no longer wrote for it on a regular basis.[36] Although like Lever a model employer renowned for his philanthropy, Cadbury was 'a cad and coward' to Chesterton because like other newspaper proprietors, he was too timid to fight powerful vested interests and real abuses. Chesterton's alienation from the press was con-

---

[34.] Maisie Ward, *Gilbert Keith Chesterton*, p. 256.

[35.] G. K. Chesterton, 'The Song of Right and Wrong', *Collected Poems*, p. 218.

[36.] Joseph Pearce, *Wisdom and Innocence: A Life of G. K. Chesterton*, London, Hodder & Stoughton, 1996, p. 186.

firmed by the prosecution of his brother Cecil for alleging corruption in the Liberal administration over insider share dealings in what was known as the Marconi scandal. The Marconi scandal was a complicated affair, in which Chesterton was not wholly in the right, but it involved the future Liberal Prime Minister, David Lloyd George, under whom one species of corruption was to achieve heroic proportions, the government's sale of peerages to benefit the Liberal Party.

The sanctimony of the liberal proprietor of the *Daily News* no doubt suggested one part of Chesterton's wonderful portrait in *The Flying Inn* of the editor Hibbs, the master of the irrelevant but high-sounding non sequitur: Hibbs, a minor antihero in a work devoted to a conspiracy to make England Muslim and teetotal, only becomes human when he gets drunk. Like Chesterton's millionaires, like Mr Mandragon, a vegetarian who symbolically ate men, Hibbs was a puritan who has no idea of how to enjoy himself, and only takes to the bottle for the worst of reasons, from worry and the wish for oblivion.

Yet Chesterton also had his model of the journalist as hero. His own particular great man was the uncrowned king of British journalists, the militant early nineteenth-century farmer-editor William Cobbett, who, in Chesterton's words, was 'the noblest English example of the noble calling of the agitator',[37] a writer, fighter and biter for whom journalism was properly the mouthpiece of the poor and the journalist was the tribune of the people.

Cobbett was himself a radical, but was also a Tory traditionalist believing in the ancient English virtues. Though a devout if eirenic anticlerical Protestant and a member of the Church of England, in his *History of the Protestant Reformation*, he took the findings of the very moderate Catholic historian John Lingard and turned them into a flaming sword in the hands of non-Catholic radicals like himself. Thus Cobbett idealised the medieval Catholic past as Merrie England, and the Reformation as the era of the pillage of the

---

[37.] G. K. Chesterton, 'Introduction', *Cottage Economy by William Cobbett*, London, Douglas Pepler, 1916, p. iii.

Church and of the monasteries and therefore of the patri-
mony of the poor. In Chesterton's view, Cobbett stood for
England: England unindustrialised, self-sufficient, relying
on a basis of agriculture and sound commerce. Cobbett had
'denounced the eating up of England by factories and industrial towns',[38] the destruction of the England of bacon and
beer, and cakes and ale, of tumbledown hovels and cottage
gardens, the Little England of a pre-imperial English nation-
alism, an England sufficient in itself and utterly indifferent
to that whole ideal of the greater Britain or British Empire
which was the religion of the Australia of my childhood.

Chesterton particularly rejoiced in Cobbett's demonstra-
tion of the resources of the English language for abusing
others, and he mourned the decay of this instrument in his
own time, when the people who should be roundly abused
so richly abounded. Chesterton was the least practical of
men, but he also delighted in Cobbett's exposition in his
Cottage Economy of the arts of the English countryside,
in brewing beer, keeping cows, pigs and poultry, making
mustard, plaiting straw for hats and bonnets and growing the
Indian maize which Cobbett himself had brought back from
America. Cobbett understood the England of Everyman, of
the ordinary Englishman, above all of the mass of the population who were still in his day agricultural labourers, who
often went hungry, an England the very knowledge of which
was now denied by the English press to the English people.

Here, therefore, was a tremendous paradox at the heart of
Chesterton's view of England and the English: that popular
literature, the press which the people read, had been entirely
corrupted by its rich proprietors and by their dependent
lackeys in his own profession, while the professors, who
might at least have created a true history of England, had
written histories from which the English people were absent
altogether. Chesterton's distrust of journalism was, however,
to be greatly enhanced by his developing Catholicism, with
its story of a primordial fall away of the country from true
religion and from its boasted medieval claim to be the Virgin
Mary's dowry. Chesterton's interpretation of English history

38. Ibid.

was informed by his concomitant social philosophy, based upon Pope Leo XIII's body of teaching on the sanctity of private property, which should be as widely available as possible, especially among the peasantry. The influence of Leo on Chesterton came with his adoption of Hilaire Belloc's 'distributist' affirmation of the virtues of peasant proprietorship and small-scale businesses and craft unions or guilds as the economic foundation of a properly Catholic social order. Distributism was for Chesterton the Catholic alternative to the unregulated capitalism and the over-regulated communism which between them would lay waste the world. Chesterton was, moreover, a convert to Hilaire Belloc's view of the Servile State, and to Belloc's rejection of the Liberal Party's use of the State, even in a charitable fashion, to make dependent slaves of its citizens, through the State provision of health care and old age pensions.

In this, Chesterton's theology was from the first a liberation theology, but a liberation theology with a difference. Chesterton's lack of belief in the State and his belief in property ownership separated him by a great gulf from the politicians of the conventional British left, with whom he otherwise had so much in common. They wanted a propertyless proletariat to rebel to create a Socialist State; he wanted the poor to rise, but to abolish the State and become propertied.

But the English poor owned nothing, and so Chesterton's vision of English history, as a conspiracy of rich men against poor ones, has a shadow resemblance to vulgar Marxism, and to its belief in the long and successful campaign of the rich to hide the truth from the people. Marxists declared that the party system of Liberal against Conservative in late Victorian and Edwardian England was a sham contest between rival bodies of oligarchs and plutocrats. Chesterton, and his brother Cecil, and Belloc, perfectly agreed with them.

This is, in fact, an exaggeration: there were real issues in British party politics which deeply divided the Liberals and the Tories, as over the reform of the House of Lords and Home Rule for Ireland. But Chesterton's revulsion from modern plutocratic England informs the vision of his *A Short History of England*, in which the central occurrence

is not so much even the Reformation, as a series of social
and economic events from which the Reformation profited,
the destruction of the popular culture of medieval or Merrie
England: the dispossession of its yeomen farmers to create
sheep walks; the suppression of the incipient democracy of
the Peasants' Revolt and of the guilds, which had anticipated
the modern trade unions; the enclosure of the common
lands on which the poor could graze a pig or cow; the
transfer of the properties of the monasteries to a new race
of squires, and the sacrifice of the poor to the harsh aus-
terities of the Tudor Poor Laws. The Reformation fostered
the creation of the squirearchy and then of industrialism, in
that interaction of Protestantism with the rise of capitalism
expounded by Max Weber and R. H. Tawney.

Some parts of this picture have a long history: Chesterton's
anti-industrialism was a large part of Romanticism. England,
the oldest of the industrial nations, has the strongest attach-
ment to its rural landscapes, and contains the world's most
dedicated flower and vegetable gardeners, and although the
nation was the first in history in which a majority of people
came to live in the towns, its heart still lies in a thatched
cottage in the country. The hostile reaction against the
factory system occurred in both ultra-conservatives and
ultra-radicals, and in such nineteenth-century writers as
Robert Southey, Augustus Pugin, John Ruskin and Thomas
Carlyle, the last of whom coined the phrase the 'gloomy
science' to describe the kind of political economy which justified industrialism and the doctrines of liberal laissez-faire.
Chesterton's understanding of English history is the sinister
one to be found among backward-looking Socialists such as
the great artist and designer William Morris, who deplored
the replacement of medieval craftsmanship and local materials by mass production, as well as among the high Tory
clergy of the Oxford Movement, who wanted a return to
the rule of benevolent medieval priests. It is an essentially
English vision. Above all, this was the vision of Cobbett, a
prophet who foresaw the modern world as we know it now:

> the perishing of the whole English power of self-support, the
> growth of cities that drain and dry up the countryside, the

growth of dense dependent populations incapable of finding their own food, the toppling triumph of machines over men, the sprawling omnipotence of financiers over patriots, the herding of humanity in nomadic masses whose very homes are homeless, the terrible necessity of peace and the terrible probability of war, all the loading up of our little island like a sinking ship; the wealth that may mean famine and the culture that may mean despair ...[39]

This is an understanding of the past entirely opposed to the dominant tradition of English historiography, the Whig interpretation of English history as a story of progress through Protestantism, the Enlightenment and industrialism to the great cities, riches and liberalism of the present. Indeed Chesterton's view is equally opposed to the countervailing power of Agatha Christie's rival Tory vision of England in the Miss Marple detective stories, said to be the best-selling books in the world after the Bible, which have as background the village of St Mary Mead, with its parson and squire, a traditional rural England to which murder comes as the violation by the murderer of a perfect social and moral order. Against both the Whigs and the Tories, Chesterton saw the history of England not as a progress upward from medieval barbarism to a pleasant present and a better future, or as the conservation of a much-loved tradition, but as a long descent to the pit and the everlasting bonfire.

Like Cobbett before him, and Pugin and Carlyle, Chesterton exaggerated the charity of the medieval monasteries – poor relief was essentially a parochial responsibility – and he simplified English history into a story of decline and fall. But one strand of his argument has been legitimated by recent scholars like Eamon Duffy, in their picture of the genuine popularity of late medieval Catholicism, which only

---

[39.] G. K. Chesterton, *William Cobbett*, London, Hodder & Stoughton, 1925, pp. 14–15.

the English Crown could destroy.[40] Chesterton thought that the English masses had never become fully Protestant, though here it is possible that he underestimated the place in popular consciousness of a negative No Popery, the anti-Catholic British tradition, with its burnings of effigies of the pope every 5 November. To Chesterton, the decay of peasant proprietorship had heralded the advent of the dark satanic mills of the factory system and all its woes, and the worst exploitation by the rich of the poor in history, with their concomitant oppression in the nineteenth-century workhouses of the New Poor Law, which imprisoned the destitute for their destitution. Chesterton's history is as present-minded as Marx's, as an explanation of the evils of the industrial present and of the condition of the urban poor.

But Chesterton's democratic faith, forged by his love of the poetry of Whitman and Browning, and confirmed by Belloc's enthusiasm for the French Revolution, which Belloc and Chesterton wrongly thought had endowed the French peasantry with property, left him with the problem as to why it was only in a cosmetic sense that England had become a democracy, unlike countries reborn in the fires of real revolutions, like the United States and France and Ireland. The central facts of recent British history were that England had escaped the French Revolution, and that the English poor, in the army of Wellington and the navy of Nelson, had fought like lions against France to keep themselves in chains. Chesterton's poem, 'The Secret People', is still often quoted, as on the Internet, in support of allegations of conspiracy by cliques and cabals against the public good, and it portrays the poor as essentially passive spectators to the better-known currents of public events, so that where conventional Socialist and radical historians have exaggerated the revolutionary possibilities of the Chartist and Labour movements, Chesterton quickly passes over them, for none of them had been successful.

[40.] Eamon Duffy, *The Stripping of the Altars: Traditional Religion in England c.1400–c.1580*, New Haven and London, Yale University Press, 1992.

And yet for all their sufferings, and in spite of their apparent willingness to be dupes, Chesterton insisted that the English poor had not been corrupted. Not of course that he believed in their original virtue: he had too profound a grasp of the doctrine of Original Sin. Yet the 'Secret People' retain a mysterious innocence:

> Smile at us, pay us, pass us; but do not quite forget;
> For we are the people of England, that never have spoken yet.
> There is many a fat farmer that drinks less cheerfully,
> There is many a free French peasant who is richer and sadder
> than we.
> There are no folk in the whole world so helpless or so wise.
> There is hunger in our bellies, there is laughter in our eyes;
> You laugh at us and love us, both mugs and eyes are wet:
> Only you do not know us. For we have not spoken yet.[41]

There is, therefore, an undercurrent of menace in the poem. The people retain at least the possibility of revolutionary action, and their masters, who 'look at our labour and laughter as a tired man looks at flies', should fear them:

> It may be we shall rise the last as Frenchmen rose the first,
> Our wrath come after Russia's wrath and our wrath be the
> worst.[42]

It should perhaps be noted that the wrath of Russia referred to here was not the Bolshevik rising of 1917, for the poem was published before then, in 1915, but the aborted revolution of 1905. This enthusiasm for red revolution should give the lie to the absurd assertion that Chesterton was some sort of fascist. He was an anti-elitist, a populist, a democrat heart and soul, and an occasionally bloody-minded one, as in his regret that Britain had experienced no civil war since the seventeenth century. He was convinced that 'the meanest man is immortal', as made in the divine image. He respected the people even when they became a mob. But why the English should have been so unaffected at their heart by

---

41. 'The Secret People', *Collected Poems*, p. 173.
42. G. K. Chesterton, *Collected Poems*, p. 176.

five hundred years of passivity remains unclear, except
through a kind of faith, Chesterton's unshakeable faith in
the virtue and immortality of the common man. They bear
their servitude with heroic fortitude to oppressors who do
not understand them. In a remarkable passage in his *A Short
History of England*, Chesterton suggests that the true secret
of the secret people is their sense of humour:

> This is the colour and the character that has run through the
> realities of English history, and it can hardly be put in a book,
> least of all a historical book. It has its flashes in our fantastic
> fiction and in the songs of the street, but its true medium is con-
> versation. It has no name but incongruity. An illogical laughter
> survives everything in the English soul. It survived, perhaps,
> with only too much patience, the time of terrorism in which
> the more serious Irish rose in revolt. That time was full of a
> quite topsy-turvey tyranny, and the English humorist stood on
> his head to suit it. Indeed, he often receives a quite irrational
> sentence in a police court by saying he will do it on his head.
> So, under Pitt's coercionist regime, a man was sent to prison
> for saying that George IV was fat; but we feel he must have been
> partly sustained in prison by the artistic contemplation of how
> fat he was. That sort of liberty, that sort of humanity, and it is no
> mean sort, did indeed survive all the drift and downward eddy
> of an evil economic system, as well as the dragooning of a reac-
> tionary epoch and the drearier menace of materialistic social
> science, as embodied in the new Puritans, who have purified
> themselves even of religion.[43]

It was humour which kept the heart of the Englishman pure
and free. If what he reads now is anything to judge him
by, I cannot think that Chesterton's faith in him could still
survive.

A saint need not be infallible in his social and political
opinions, though Chesterton's rather radical views, with
their undercurrent of revolutionary violence, might well be
cited as an obstacle to his canonisation. His sins, if they be
such, are partly those of his profession, though his compul-
sion to communicate what he saw so clearly is a partial reply

[43.] G. K. Chesterton, *A Short History of England*, London, Chatto &
Windus, 1917, pp. 221–2.

to the charge that he produced too much. The demands of journalism for copy can be insatiable, and some of what he wrote was dross. But as has been said, he threw his genius around, like gold pieces,[44] and there is gold somewhere in everything he wrote. Perhaps the greatness of a journalist can lie in his indifference to his own output, and his willingness to see it die. Chesterton was a journalist who was utterly indifferent to the ambition which moves some writers, the hope of literary immortality. Like Cobbett before him, he was more interested in his causes than in himself, and more interested in mankind than in either. In this also he stands in a tradition, a Catholic one. The nineteenth-century Catholic revival produced some great self-sacrificing, often bigoted, lion-like, populist lay journalists: Louis Veuillot in France, Orestes Brownson in the United States, Frederick Lucas in England. No profession is so important; no profession is in greater need of sanctity. But if the Church needs a patron of journalism, to stand above her altars, then the greatest of these is Chesterton.

---

[44] A. L. Maycock, *The Man who was Orthodox*, roughly citing Robert Lynd, p. 13.

Appendix A

The Philosemitism of G. K. Chesterton

William Oddie

The accusation that Chesterton was an anti-Semite, which has in recent years surfaced from time to time, was vividly restated in *The New Yorker* in July 2008 by Adam Gopnik. According to Gopnik, G. K. Chesterton had an 'ugly' and 'obsessive' hatred of Jews. Gopnik claims to be an admirer of Chesterton. He writes:

> Chesterton is a difficult writer to defend, [t]hose of us who are used to pressing his writing on friends have the hard job of protecting him from his detractors, who think he was a nasty anti-Semite and medievalising reactionary, and the still harder one of protecting him from his admirers, who *pretend* that he was not [my italics].

Gopnik has his own agenda: he claims, for instance, that Chesterton's supposed Jew-hatred was linked to his conversion to Catholicism, saying he was attracted by the Church's 'authoritarian and poetic solutions' and therefore went for its allegedly endemic anti-Semitism too. But there is more: '[i]t's a *deeply racial*, not merely religious, bigotry; it's not the Jews' cupidity or their class role – it's them' [My italics]. The trouble for 'those of us who love Chesterton's writing', he argues, 'is that the anti-Semitism is not incidental: it rises from the logic of his poetic position'. This leads Gopnik to some quite grotesque accusations: in one way, this is useful, since it demonstrates clearly how profoundly ignorant he is of Chesterton's real beliefs. Gopnik ludicrously claims that he dreamed of an anti-capitalist agricultural state overseen by the Catholic Church and governed by a military for whom medieval ideas of honour still resonated, a place where Jews would not be persecuted or killed, certainly, but hived off and always marked as foreigners ... his ideal order was ascendant over the whole Iberian Peninsula for half a century.

This almost answers itself: Chesterton demonstrably believed in nothing remotely like this authoritarian, centralising, anti-localist, clericalist and militarist nightmare.

The best place to begin, perhaps, is with the accusation against Chesterton of an obsessive and *racially based* loathing of Jews, since the question of race (with its connections with Eugenics and its goal of racial purity[1] – a pseudo-science of which Chesterton was virtually the only major opponent) is fundamental to the 'anti-Semitism' of Chesterton's lifetime. The term was invented around 1873 by Wilhelm Marr to describe the policy toward Jews based on 'Racism' that he and others advocated. The theory asserted that 'humans were divided into clearly distinguishable races and that the intellectual, moral and social conduct and potential of the members of these races were biologically determined. As elaborated in the Aryan myth, it maintained that Jews were a race and that, not only were they, like other races, inferior to the Aryan race, but also that Jews were the most dangerous of those inferior races'.[2] In 1879 Marr founded the League of Antisemites (Antisemiten-Liga), the first German organisation committed specifically to combating the alleged threat to Germany posed by the Jews and advocating their forced removal from the country. He was probably influenced by Ernst Haeckel (ridiculed during the Blatchford controversy by Chesterton) who popularised the notion of Social Darwinism in Germany.

Chesterton was, in fact, brusquely impatient of current

[1.] Fr Saward (p. 26 above) quotes the assertion of H. G. Wells (one of many contemporary supporters of Eugenics) that the 'swarms of black, and brown, and dirty-white, and yellow people, who do not come into the new needs of efficiency', will 'have to go'.

[2.] Gavin I. Langmuir, *Toward a Definition of Antisemitism*, University of California Press, Berkeley, 1990, p. 311.

(and widespread) ideas about racial superiority; in 1925 he wrote:

> I shall begin to take seriously those classifications of superiority
> and inferiority, when I find a man classifying himself as inferior
> It is so with the men who talk about superior and inferior races;
> I never heard a man say: Anthropology shows that I belong to
> an inferior race. If he did, he might be talking like an anthro-
> pologist; as it is, he is talking like a man, and not infrequently
> like a fool.[3]

In 1934, he wrote in *GK's Weekly* that 'the stupidest thing done', not simply in 1933 but 'in the last two or three centuries, was the acceptance by the Germans of the Dictatorship of Hitler', who had risen to power not 'by enunciating a certain theory of the state' but by 'appealing to racial pride'. It was, he wrote, 'staggering' that 'a whole huge people should base its whole historical tradition on something that is not so much a legend as a lie'. The 'Teutonic Theory' was the invention of professors; the 'strange staleness' of this 'racial religion' stank with 'the odours of decay, and of something dug up when it was dead and buried'.[4]

Thus, not only was Chesterton not a racist, he was positively and with deliberation intellectually hostile to the philosophy underlying 'racism' and hence to that underlying its derivative, 'anti-semitism'. But we need to say more: as a matter of historic record, he had, quite simply, too many genuine and sometimes profound friendships for too many individual Jews throughout his lifetime for the charge even of a general dislike of or distaste for Jews – let alone of Gopnik's fanatical charge that he was a 'Jew-hater' whose hatreds were 'ugly and obsessive' – to be even remotely plausible. On any occasion of discrimination against or cruelty towards Jews – whether individual or collective – he was, instinctively, firmly on the Jewish side. As he puts it in his *Autobiography*, 'I lived to have later on the name of an

---

[3.] *GK's Weekly*, 25 April 1925.
[4.] G. K. Chesterton, *The End of the Armistice*, ed. Frank Sheed, London, Sheed & Ward, 1940, pp. 559ff.

Anti-Semite; whereas from my first days at school I very largely had the name of a Pro-Semite ... I was criticised in early days for quixotry and priggishness in protecting Jews', a reference to his schooldays habit of intervening when boys were being bullied for being Jewish. Chesterton's *Autobiography* is not always a reliable source; but there is considerable corroborating evidence for these protective feelings from his childhood onwards: and since this evidence is virtually unknown, it is probably best here to take this opportunity to publish it again (much of it appeared in my book *Chesterton and the Romance of Orthodoxy*, though I discovered some of it too late for it to be included).

Some of this evidence is to be found in the notebooks which he kept from his childhood until the end of his life. In one notebook, he kept an unfortunately short-lived diary, in which he recorded his strong feelings about Russian oppression of the Jews, feelings which had been triggered off by reading in a magazine article of the case of a 'respectable young girl of honest parents' who had been seduced by a Christian who had promised to marry her. When she reminded him of his promise, he replied that 'he would have her sent out of the city for her presumption. And he did. A cousin of his is serving in the police department, and he had no difficulty to obtain an order for her banishment as a disorderly Jewess. But how could you bring yourself to do such a damnable act? [the article's author] asked. Oh, she is only a Jewess! he answered. What else is she good for? Besides, everybody else does the same'.[5] Chesterton's reaction was explosive:

[Diary. Monday Jan 5th, 1891]
Expect Bentley. Read in Review of Reviews. Various revelation[s] of Jews in Russia. Brutal falsehood and cruelty to a Jewish girl. Made me feel strongly inclined to knock some-body down, but refrained.

Chesterton's feelings about Russian anti-Semitism were reflected in a series of pieces published during 1891 (written

5. *Review of Reviews*, October 1890, ii, no 10, 350.

in the form of fictional Letters) in The Debater, the school
magazine of which he was co-founder and a prolific con-
tributor:

> [*Debater*, iii, 11]
> What do you think of the persecution of the Jews in Russia? It
> has, at least, done one service to orthodoxy. It has restored my
> belief in the Devil.

> [*Debater*, iii, 29]
> I am going to Russia, I think the most godless, hell-darkened
> place I can think of, to see if I can't ... help the Hebrews ... or
> do something else that will be for the good of humanity.

The series comes to a dramatic end with a fictional letter,
written as though from St Petersburg, in which Chesterton's
alter ego, 'Guy Crawford', describes himself as joining a
rebellious mob in which he recognises an obviously Jewish
student called Emmanuel, and as springing to his defence,
sword in hand, as the Czarist troops attack: but Emmanuel
sustains a fatal blow and dies in the street, 'a champion of
justice, like thousands who have fallen for it in the dark
records of this dark land'.[6]
At about the same time, he wrote a poem entitled 'Before
a statue of Cromwell', a tribute to Cromwell's positive
response in 1656 to a petition for the readmission of Jews to
England. Cromwell is pointedly held up as a noble contrast
to Russia's current rulers:

> O thou grim old captain, watching from the land before the
> grave
> Like a wounded king and warrior, all the strivings of the brave.
> You that work the will of Russia, howling Christ against the few
> He will take some crowd of heathen ere He opens the gates to
> you
> Christ has borne from you more insult than from Israel he has
> borne
> Ye have placed the scourge of murder where they placed the
> reed of scorn[7]

6. *The Debater*, iii, 71.
7. *Works*, vol. x (Collected Poetry, part 1), San Francisco, Ignatius Press,
1994, p. 28.

This dates from around 1892. Czarist Russia was not his only target; later in the decade he wrote a poem entitled 'To a certain Nation', a shocked reaction to the Dreyfus affair, even at the time seen as a classic symbolic expression of European ant-Semitism, of an ingrained hostility even to culturally assimilated Jews like Dreyfus. Like many Jews, Chesterton was particularly shocked that it should be France, the homeland of liberty and the Great Revolution (he was a passionate supporter of the French Republican tradition) that had encompassed so grotesque an injustice, and wrote of his

> shame to hear, where Danton died,
> Thy foul dead kings all laughing in their graves

And continued

> Thou hast a right to rule thyself; to be
> The thing thou wilt; to grin, to fawn, to creep;
> To crown these clumsy liars; ay, and we
> Who knew thee once, we have a right to weep.

Chesterton's feelings of extreme hostility to persecutions of the Jewish people were maintained throughout his life, and were in no way modified by his feelings about Jewish plutocracy where it existed, or about certain individual Jews: towards the end of his life he wrote that he was 'appalled by the Hitlerite atrocities' (he died in 1936 before anyone knew of the full extent of what was to become the Nazi attempt at a 'final solution'):

> They have absolutely no reason or logic behind them. It is quite obviously the expedient of a man who has been driven to seeking a scapegoat, and has found with relief the most famous scapegoat in European history, the Jewish people.

As a Jewish convert to Catholicism, Michael Coren points out, '[O]pposition to the new order was not fashionable in the early days, and the people who stood up firmly against National Socialism were as righteous as they were few. Gilbert was such a man.' Chesterton wrote contemptuously, of the Nazi policy of excising Jews from German cultural history, that 'they will find it difficult to persuade any German, let alone any European who is fond of Germany that Schiller is a poet and Heine is not'; and with angry disgust of the 'thousands of Jews [who] have recently been rabbled or ruined or driven from their homes' and of the fact that 'They beat and bully poor Jews in concentration camps [this predated, of course, the policy of mass extermination] ... Heartily ... I do indeed despise the Hitlerites.' Coren quotes the view of the Wiener Library, the archive of anti-semitism in London, that he was not 'seriously anti-semitic', though he 'played along' and therefore 'has the public reputation of anti-semitism'. However, 'He was not an enemy, and when the real testing time came along he showed what side he was on.'[8]

The year after Chesterton's death, the American Rabbi Wise wrote to Cyril Clemens:

> He as Catholic, I as Jew, could not have seen eye to eye with each other ... but I deeply respected him. When Hitlerism came, he was one of the first to speak out with all the directness and frankness of a great and unabashed spirit. Blessing to his memory![9]

The youthful Chesterton had personal reasons for feeling strongly about cruelty to the Jews in Russia. Of the twelve members of the Junior Debating Club – the exclusive membership of which was determined by Chesterton and by his friends Bentley and Oldershaw – four were Jewish: the Solomons, Lawrence and Maurice and the D'Avigdors, Digby and Waldo. Chesterton stayed with the Solomon family during at least one school vacation; Lawrence Solomon was to be a lifelong friend, who even moved to Beaconsfield in Chesterton's wake so as to be near him; he and his wife were frequent visitors to Chesterton's house.

Chesterton's view of Jews in general was exactly that of the Zionist movement: that Jews were exiles, and would never be happy until they had their own country. Chester-

8. Michael Coren, *Gilbert: The Man Who Was Chesterton*, London, Jonathan Cape, 1989, p. 210.
9. Maisie Ward, *Gilbert Keith Chesterton*, London, Sheed and Ward, 1945, p. 228.

ton simply thought (a normal opinion at the time, in the wake of a recent wave of Jewish immigration) that Jews were foreigners who had no desire to lose their separate identity: the 'Jewish problem', in the words of Theodore Herzl, the founding father of Zionism (who had been radicalised by the experience of reporting the Dreyfus affair), was that 'We are aliens here, they do not let us dissolve into the popula-tion, *and if they let us we would not do it*. Let us go forth! [My italics]'[10]

Chesterton, indeed, claimed to be a Zionist himself. He once explained this (to a Jewish audience) by saying that 'While all other races had local attachments, the Jews were universal and scattered. They could not be expected to have patriotism for the countries in which they made their homes.'[11] This view may be disputable (time has certainly made it so); but it is not anti-Semitic. Chesterton's claim to be a Zionist may seem eccentric to us: but, again, it is hardly anti-Semitic: nor was it unusual (there was at the time a well-established tradition of Christian Zionism, of which A. J. Balfour is the most obvious example). During his journey to Palestine in 1919, Chesterton had lunch with Chaim Weizmann, later the first President of Israel: Weizmann would certainly have sniffed out an anti-Semite if Chesterton had actually been one. The resulting book, *The New Jerusalem* sums up Chesterton's view:

> If the Jew cannot be at ease in Zion [a reference to Amos 6:1: 'Woe to them that are at ease in Zion'] we can never again persuade ourselves that he is at ease out of Zion. We can only salute as it passes that restless and mysterious figure, knowing at last that there must be in him something mystical as well as mysterious; that whether in the sense of the sorrows of Christ or of the sorrows of Cain, he must pass by, for he belongs to God.

The New Jerusalem, however, poses a problem: for, though it can certainly be seen as evidence for Chesterton's Zionism

---

[10.] Alex Bein, *Theodore Herzl, a biography*, trans. Maurice Samuel, Cleveland, World Pub. Co., 1962, p. 162.

[11.] Maisie Ward, *Gilbert Keith Chesterton*, pp. 227–8.

and for his appreciation of the 'mystical as well as mysterious' dimension of the Jewish heritage, it also contains
passages which explain why Gopnik perceives Chesterton's
agreement with the Zionist's perception that 'we are aliens
here' in a sinister light. At one point, Chesterton seeks to
explain his feeling that Jews are foreigners and should not
take on the airs of the English establishment (undoubtedly
thinking of the galling attainment by his arch-enemy from
the Marconi affair, Rufus Isaacs, of the position of head of
the English judiciary by indulging in a joke: a joke, however
which from our own historical standpoint has turned sour:

> Let a Jew be Lord Chief Justice if his exceptional veracity and
> reliability have clearly marked him out for that post [Isaacs's
> proven gross corruption, does in fact, by today's standards,
> make his judicial ascent seem astonishing]. Let a Jew be Arch-
> bishop of Canterbury ... But let there be one single-clause bill
> [enacting] that every Jew must be dressed like an Arab ... If my
> image is quaint my intention is quite serious ... The point is
> that we should know where we are; and he would know where
> he is, which is in a foreign land.

'Hitler', says Gopnik, 'made a simpler demand for Jewish
dress, *but the idea was the same.*' But 'the idea' ABSOLUTELY
WAS *NOT* THE SAME: Hitler wanted the Jews identified so that
they could be first dispossessed and then annihilated:
Chesterton wanted them to be given special privileges and
protection. As Ian Ker discusses in his biography of Chesterton, he 'favoured not only a home for the Jews in Palestine,
but if possible an "extension of the definition of Zionism"
that would "overcome ... the difficulty of resettling a sufficient number of so large a race on so small a land": namely,
by giving Jews who did not live in the national homeland "a
special position best described as a privilege; some sort of
self-governing enclave with special laws and exemptions"'.
As Ker[12] rightly objects, this 'extension' of Zionism would
simply have created the 'kind of ghetto that had facilitated
the persecution of Jews'; but this, he suggests, 'cannot be

[12.] Ian Ker, *G. K. Chesterton: A Biography*, Oxford University Press; due
for publication in April 2011.

said was Chesterton's intention which sounds perfectly sincere even if quite impractical – or worse'.

Better to understand Chesterton's idea that Jews were not naturally a part of English culture without perceiving it through the inevitably determinative intervening lens of the Nazi holocaust; we might compare it with modern English perceptions of the problem of multiculturalism as it applies particularly to the Moslem community, still widely seen as being impossible to assimilate (particularly in view of the clearly separatist attitudes of many influential Muslims, whose thinking is very like that of Theodore Herzl, that 'we are aliens here … and if they let us we would not [dissolve into the population]': thus, there is understood by many decent and tolerant people to be what might be termed a 'Moslem problem' (just as many decent and tolerant gentiles in Chesterton's day thought, as the Zionists did, that there was a 'Jewish problem'). The perspective of history may or may not similarly show this 'problem' too to be illusory.

Gopnik dismisses Chesterton's claim to be a Zionist by saying that many anti-Semites cynically made the same claim, as a kind of polemical trick (though he gives no evidence for this assertion). But Chesterton was entirely sincere, as Weizmann probably perceived; and by the time he visited Palestine he had held these views for at least three decades. In one of Chesterton's youthful notebooks, which we can date around 1893, he recorded the following pensée: *'No Christian ought to be an anti-semite. But every Christian ought to be a Zionist.'* His Zionism, that is to say, is defined here in the context of the hostility to anti-Semitism which he had recently expressed in his diary and in the poems and *Debater* articles I have quoted. The terms 'Zionism' and 'Zionist' had in fact been coined only three years before; and Chesterton's use of it predates the existence of an actual Zionist movement: the first Zionist Congress took place in 1897. Thus, we can say that this was a question that had engaged him from the beginning: and that his understanding of what Zionists too called 'the Jewish problem' was from the outset determined in the context of his *hostility* to anti-Semitism.

Chesterton explained these Zionist views in 1911 to a

Jewish audience (it is worth asking, in passing, whether it is likely that any anti-Semite would have accepted an invitation to address such an audience). Maisie Ward records:

> Speaking at the Jewish West End Literary Society he put the question of what the real Jewish problem was. The Jews, he said, were a race, born civilised. You never met a Jewish clod or yokel. They represented one of the highest of civilised types. But while all other races had local attachments, the Jews were universal and scattered. They could not be expected to have patriotism for the countries in which they made their homes: their patriotism could be only for their race. In principle, he believed in the solution of Zionism. And then the reporter in large letters made a headline: 'Mr. Chesterton said that speaking generally, *as with most other communities*, "THE POOR JEWS WERE NICE AND THE RICH WERE NASTY."'[13] [My italics]

That Chesterton made a very clear distinction between Jewish plutocrats, who he thought exercised (like all plutocrats) too much power by means of their great wealth, and Jews who were more vulnerable through their poverty is quite clear. The same year as he addressed the West End Literary Society, he wrote to a Jewish correspondent, Leslie Claude Greenberg,

> Jews (being landless) unnaturally alternate between too much power and too little ... the Jew millionaire is too safe and the Jew pedlar too harassed ... I don't mind how fiercely you fight for the pedlar.

This effectively answers Gopnik's accusation that 'it's not the Jews' cupidity or their class role – it's them', by making it clear that it was indeed Jews of a particular class that he disliked: that is, rich Jews who might be accused (as 'POOR JEWS' who 'WERE NICE' could not) of 'cupidity'.[14]

This occasion, of course was pre-Marconi: and almost certainly, it looks back to Chesterton's support for the Boers during the South African War, a conflict which was widely (and not entirely without justification) seen at the time by

13. Maisie Ward, *Gilbert Keith Chesterton*, pp. 227–8.
14. G. K. Chesterton to Leslie Claude Greenberg, 26 April 1911, BL MSS Add. 73237, f.109. I am grateful to Dr Ian Ker for drawing my attention to this letter.

those opposed to the war, especially on the left, as having been fomented by Jewish financial interests. The Labour MP, John Burns, declared in the House of Commons, as the war raged, that 'Wherever we [look], there is the financial Jew, operating, directing, inspiring the agencies that have led to this war.'[15] This was certainly a paranoid overstatement: it is nevertheless undoubtedly the case that gold mining interests (notably in the person of Alfred Beit, a friend of Milner, who conspired with Cecil Rhodes in the Jameson raid, which he partly financed) were actively involved in encouraging the cause of anti-Boer interests in South Africa and the imperialist cause in general; and of the six largest mining companies, four were controlled by Jews, one of whom was Beit himself.[16] Chesterton's passionate advocacy of the Boer cause, together with a general distaste for plutocracy, thus undoubtedly fed his feeling that *rich* Jews 'were nasty'.

What, then, are we to conclude about the widespread modern view that Chesterton was an 'anti-semite'? As we have seen, 'anti-semitism' is inextricably bound up with 'racism': it is not possible to be an 'anti-semite' without accepting the underlying assumptions of 'racism' as first expounded by Wilhelm Marr; and as we have seen Chesterton's attitude to the notion that one race might be superior or inferior to another, or that a particular race might be intrinsically undesirable in some way, was one of unambiguous disgust: he believed, it will be recalled, that the 'racial religion' of the Nazis stank with 'the odours of decay, and of something dug up when it was dead and buried'.[17] If Chesterton was anti-Jewish in any way, concludes Dr Ker,

> He was anti-Jewish in exactly the same kind of way that many Europeans are anti-American today, or that Irish Americans

---

[15.] Claire Hirshfield, 'The Boer War and the Issue of Jewish Responsibility', Pennsylvania State University, Ogontz Campus, 1978, unpublished manuscript, pp. 10, 20.

[16.] G. Saron and L. Hotz, (eds), *The Jews in South Africa: a History*, London, Oxford University Press, 1955, pp. 193–4.

[17.] G. K. Chesterton, *The End of the Armistice*, pp. 559ff.

are or used to be anti-British, or that British people were anti-German and anti-Japanese after the Second World War ... But whereas, Chesterton himself complained, people were 'allowed to express ... general impressions' about the Irish or the Scots or Yorkshiremen' this latitude was not permitted in the case of the Jews: 'There (for some reason I have never understood), the whole natural tendency has been to stop; and anybody who says anything whatever about Jews as Jews is supposed to wish to burn them at the stake.'[18]

We need to say more: that the notion that Chesterton was *hostile* to 'Jews as Jews', that, in Gopnik's words, 'it's not the Jews' cupidity or their class role – it's them' expresses, quite simply, the reverse of the truth. On the contrary: there is more solid evidence for Chesterton's respect for the Jews than for his alleged anti-Semitism, even though at the same time he may express hostility to the behaviour of particular Jews in particular circumstances. In a similar way, it is possible to be anti-American when discussing foreign policy but strongly pro-American when discussing the American character or American culture. In the same way, a genuine Francophile might concede that there is such a thing as a characteristically French way of being insufferable, and more than one particularly insufferable French type. A French Anglophile would have a similarly ambiguous attitude to the English. Any 'anti-Jewish' distaste Chesterton feels is for particular Jews or for a particular class of Jews, notably plutocratic Jews: for the Jewish cultural and historical identity, on the contrary, there is respect, even reverence. With his 'salute' to 'the Jew', 'that restless and mysterious figure, knowing ... that ... he belongs to God' we can place the following passage on 'the mission ... of the Jews' (which apart from anything else refutes the notion that Chesterton's Catholicism led him to anti-Semitism) from *The Everlasting Man,* his first Catholic masterpiece: 'the meaning of the Jews', says Chesterton, was 'that the world owes God to the Jews through ... all their wanderings ...

[18.] Ian Ker, *G. K. Chesterton: A Biography*, Oxford, Oxford University Press, due for publication in April 2011. Quoting from chapter 10.

they did indeed carry the fate of the world in that wooden tabernacle':

> It would have been easy enough for his [the God of Israel's] worshippers to follow the enlightened course of Syncretism and the pooling of all the pagan traditions. It is obvious indeed that his followers were always sliding down this easy slope; and it required the almost demoniac energy of certain inspired demagogues, who testified to the divine unity in words that are still like winds of inspiration and ruin. The more we really understand of the ancient conditions that contributed to the final culture of the Faith, the more we shall have a real and even a realistic reverence for the greatness of the Prophets of Israel. As it was, while the whole world melted into this mass of confused mythology, this Deity who is called tribal and narrow, precisely because he was what is called tribal and narrow, preserved the primary religion of all mankind. He was tribal enough to be universal. He was as narrow as the universe.

So much for Gopnik's argument that Chesterton's 'national spirit' and 'extreme localism' led him to his supposed anti-Semitism: they were, in fact, precisely what gave him his respect for other nations and other cultures, and particularly for that of the Jews, to which the world owed its knowledge of God, 'as narrow as the universe'. It is the paradox of the sacramental principle, in which infinity is contained within the limited and tangible; but Adam Gopnik, resolute secularist and anti-Catholic that he is, cannot be expected to understand that.

Appendix B

The Prayer

Following the Chesterton Society's 2009 conference on the holiness of G. K. Chesterton, a prayer for his intercession was composed by one of those who attended, a layman, with the guidance of a priest. When posted on the society's blog, this evoked an immediate response. The American Chesterton Society printed several thousand copies in the form of prayer cards and distributed them. Within weeks of the prayer's posting, translations appeared in Italian and Spanish and were also posted. Indications are emerging that the prayer is being widely used, sometimes in circumstances of grave illness. The prayer is, of course, unauthorised, and should only be used privately. The texts of the prayer in English, Spanish and Italian are as follows:

Prayer for the intercession of Gilbert Chesterton

God our Father,
You filled the life of your servant Gilbert Keith Chesterton with a sense of wonder and joy, and gave him a faith which was the foundation of his ceaseless work, a hope which sprang from his enduring gratitude for the gift of human life, and a charity towards all men, particularly his opponents.

May his innocence and his laughter, his constancy in fighting for the Christian faith in a world losing belief, his lifelong devotion to the Blessed Virgin Mary and his love for all men, especially for the poor, bring cheerfulness to those in despair, conviction and warmth to lukewarm believers and the knowledge of God to those without faith.
We beg you to grant the favours we ask through his intercession, [and especially for] so that his holiness may be recognised by all and the Church may proclaim him Blessed.

We ask this through Christ our Lord.

Amen.

Oración por la beatificación de Chesterton

Dios nuestro Padre,
Tú que has colmado la vida de tu siervo Gilbert Keith Chesterton con ese sentido del asombro y el gozo, y le diste esa fe que fue el fundamento de su incesante trabajo, esa esperanza que nacía de su perdurable gratitud por el don de la vida humana, y esa caridad para con todos los hombres particularmente sus oponentes:

haz que su inocencia y su risa, su constancia en combatir por la fe cristiana en un mundo descreído, su devoción de toda la vida por la Santísima Virgen María y su amor por todos los hombres, especialmente por los pobres, concedan alegría a aquellos que se hallan sin esperanza, convicción y calidez a los creyentes tibios y el conocimiento de Dios a aquellos que no tienen fe.

Te rogamos otorgar los favores que te pedimos por su intercesión, [y especialmente por] de manera que su santidad pueda ser reconocida por todos y la Iglesia pueda proclamarlo Beato.

Te lo pedimos por Cristo Nuestro Señor.

Amén.

Una preghiera per l'intercessione di Gilbert Chesterton

Dio Nostro Padre,
Tu riempisti la vita del tuo servo Gilbert Keith Chesterton di un senso di meraviglia e gioia, e desti a lui una fede che fu il fondamento del suo incessante lavoro, una carità verso tutti gli uomini, in particolare verso i suoi avversari, e una speranza che scaturiva dalla sua gratitudine di un'intera vita per il dono della vita umana.

Possano la sua innocenza e e le sue risate, la sua costanza nel combattere per la fede cristiana in un mondo che perde la fede, la sua devozione di una vita per la Beata Vergine Maria e il suo amore per tutti gli uomini, specialmente per i poveri, portare allegria ai disperati, convinzione e calore ai tiepidi e la conoscenza di Dio a chi non ha fede. Ti chiediamo di concedere le grazie cheTi imploriamo attraverso la sua intercessione (e specialmente per) perché la sua santità possa essere riconosciuta da tuttie e la Chiesa possa proclamarlo beato.

Te lo chiediamo per Cristo Nostro Signore

Amen.